IN THE NAME OF ALLAH,
THE MERCIFUL,
THE MERCY-GIVING

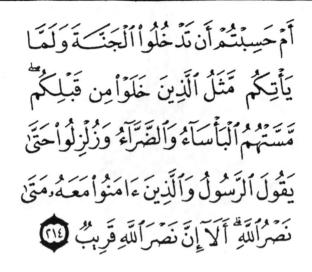

أَمْ حَسِبْتُمْ أَن تَدْخُلُوا الْجَنَّةَ وَلَمَّا
يَأْتِكُم مَّثَلُ الَّذِينَ خَلَوْا مِن قَبْلِكُم
مَّسَّتْهُمُ الْبَأْسَاءُ وَالضَّرَّاءُ وَزُلْزِلُوا حَتَّى
يَقُولَ الرَّسُولُ وَالَّذِينَ ءَامَنُوا مَعَهُ مَتَى
نَصْرُ اللَّهِ أَلَا إِنَّ نَصْرَ اللَّهِ قَرِيبٌ ﴿٢١٤﴾

Do you suppose that you will
enter Paradise untouched by the
suffering endured by the men of
faith who passed away before
you? They were afflicted by
misery and hardship and so
convulsed that the Messenger
and the believers with him cried
out: 'When will Allah's help
arrive?' They were assured that
Allah's help was close by.

(Surah al-Baqarah, 214)

Return of the Pharaoh

Memoir in Nasir's Prison

ZAINAB AL-GHAZALI

Translated by
Mokrane Guezzou

The Islamic Foundation

ISBN 0 86037 240 5

Published by
The Islamic Foundation,
Markfield Dawah Centre,
Ratby Lane, Markfield,
Leicester LE67 9RN,
United Kingdom

Quran House,
PO Box 30611,
Nairobi,
Kenya

PMB 3193,
Kano,
Nigeria

Printed in Great Britain by The Cromwell Press
Broughton Gifford, Wiltshire

Contents

Foreword   vii

Translator's Introduction   xi

Introduction   1

Chapter 1: Jamal 'Abd al-Nasir: Hatred and
    Vengeance   5
    Dealings with the Socialist Union, 8; 'NO' to
    the Despot!, 11; What Next?, 13; Bargaining
    and Deception, 14; The Night Predators, 15;
    The Many Faces of Ahmad Rasikh, 17

Chapter 2: The Pledge of Allegiance   25
    The Veil Drops, 29; Screams Calling Me to
    Duty!, 31; 'Abd al-Fattah Isma'il, 33; Permission
    to Work, 35; A Righteous Husband, 37; Contact
    with Shahid Sayyid Qutb, 39

Chapter 3: Conspiracy   43
    My Turn!, 45; The Way to Room 24, 48; Inside
    Room 24, 50; Cell No. 3, 51; The Vision, 53; But
    Allah Has United Them, 59; Back to the Vortex,
    60; The President's Envoy, 64; Dear Faces Enter
    My Cell, 66; The Death of Mustafa al-Nahhas, 68;
    Taking Food - A Form of Worship, 71; Nights of
    Torture and Bargaining, 72; Now Hamzah al-
    Basyuni's Turn, 77; Back to the Cell, 78; Another
    Night Falls, 79; A Short Break, 80; The Deadly
    Night!, 80; A Letter from Nasir, 83

Chapter 4: In the Company of Shams Badran   **87**
The Cell of Water, 91; The Crime, 95; Back to
the Cell of Water, 97; Death to the Beast!, 99;
From Mice to Water and Vice Versa, 100; From
Water to the Prosecuting Attorney, 103; The
Price of Meagre Sustenance!, 106; To Hospital,
107; In the Company of Shams!, 107; Games
for the Media, 110; Room 32, 111; Betrayal
Replaced by Loftiness, 113; Continuous
Onslaught, 116; Extracts, 117

Chapter 5: Facing Up to Nasir   **133**
It All Started as a Joke!, 135; Muhammad Qutb,
138; The Case for the Prosecution, 142; More
Torture, 144; Minced Meat, 148; Salah's
Repentance, 149; The Day of the Trial Draws
Near, 150; Glad Tidings, 152; Judgement Day,
154

Chapter 6: In Court   **159**
Greater *Jahiliyyah*, 161; Judgement is
Pronounced, 162; Moments in Allah's Pleasure,
163; The Last Bargain, 164; The Executions,
165; Last Days in the Military Prison, 166; My
Husband's Death, 167; New Neighbours, 170;
Nasir Must Stand Trial!, 170

Chapter 7: In al-Qanatir Prison, 5th June   **173**
The Nightmare, 174; A New Kind of Trial, 176;
Enemies with Humanity, 180; Death and the
Despot!, 181; Scum!, 184; A New Test, 185; The
Last Bargain, 186

Foreword

From time immemorial, Egypt has been a cradle of civilization. Its value and prestige was enhanced when Islam came to this land in the first century of Hijrah. In the course of the last 14 centuries Egypt has witnessed the rise and fall of several Islamic dynasties, and the emergence of colonialism and foreign domination, resulting in the destruction of many Islamic monuments and manifestations of Islamic history and culture. The establishment of the *Ikhwan al-Muslimun* or the 'Muslim Brotherhood' in 1928 ushered in a new era of Islamic revival and hope of liberation for the people of Egypt. However, people with vested interests in and outside Egypt could not tolerate the rise of Islam once again which in a way heralded the death of the colonial legacy and an end to the corruption and nepotism that plagued the top as well as lower ranks of the Egyptian government. Therefore, in 1949, the Supreme Guide of the movement Hasan al-Banna was assassinated, and the whole leadership of the *Ikhwan* rounded up and eliminated by imprisonment, torture, assassination and exile. Its top leaders, like 'Abd al-Qadir 'Awdah, Muhammad Farghali, and later on Sayyid Qutb and Yusuf Hawash, were hanged and many innocent followers were incarcerated in Nasir's prisons. The humiliation, torture and persecution inflicted upon thousands of innocent and defenceless people by their co-religionists is a dark chapter in the modern history of Egypt. The new Muslim rulers surpassed their colonial masters in their savagery and brutality. All this was because the *Ikhwan* and its followers wanted to restore the supremacy and glory of Islam for both themselves and for the people of Egypt.

One of the outstanding leaders of the Islamic movement of Egypt and the pace-setter of courage, piety and dedication to Islam, Zainab al-Ghazali, was a victim of this savagery and inhuman persecution. Her perseverance for the cause of Islam, her patience in the face of all kinds of affliction and persecution, her steadfastness in resisting all temptations and worldly persuasions, her courage in the face of unimaginable odds and her many qualities of head and heart remind us of the life and time of many of the Companions of the Prophet and virtuous people in earlier generations of Muslim history. Islam has produced such outstanding figures in all periods of history who not only fought the forces of evil with great courage and fortitude but also left a shining example for posterity of how to combat the forces of *Jahiliyyah* and *Taghut* and restore the glory of Islam.

In Islamic history ladies have not lagged behind in the struggle to establish truth and eradicate falsehood, to uphold Islamic values and principles, and for that matter establish Islam as a living, thriving and forward-looking religion. Zainab al-Ghazali is no exception. Although now 77 years of age and in fragile health, she is young in heart and continues to inspire young and old alike by her powerful speeches and persuasive and lucid writings.

The present book, a kind of autobiographical study highlighting the painful events of her imprisonment, is a landmark in the annals of prison memoirs and a source of inspiration and guidance for millions of people who want to see Islam thrive and flourish as a world religion, as a viable new world order and as a source of peace and happiness for all mankind. The shameful way in which Zainab al-Ghazali, a helpless lady was humiliated, persecuted and physically assaulted by the soldiers, investigators and prison officials of President Nasir defies description and imagination. Torture of criminals and hard labour for convicts are known to many people in the Third World and perhaps in the civilized world, but the type of savagery and brutality that was unashamedly unleashed on this defenceless and virtuous lady is beyond imagination. Not only human beings but ferocious dogs, serpents and mice were used to inflict ingenious forms of torture, not on a criminal, but on a lady who is, by all accounts, an embodiment of virtue, piety and modesty. Can any member of the civilized world imagine such despicable behaviour from government officials being perpetrated on their own civilians?

Zainab al-Ghazali is such a towering personality who stood like a rock, successfully thwarting mighty waves of torture and temptation. No amount of persecution and persuasion could weaken her faith and resolve in Islam. On the contrary, her determination to establish Islam as a complete code of life (*din*) not only in Egypt but all over the Muslim world increased manifold. The conversation which she had with her husband prior to her arrest by Nasir's secret police, reminding her beloved husband of the pledge he had made to her before their marriage, is a fine example of devotion to Islam and the height of commitment for the supremacy of Islam.

> '. . . let trust', she said, 'be full between us. A full trust between a man and a woman, a woman who, at the age of 18, gave her whole life to Allah and *da'wah*. *In the event of any clash between the marriage contract's interest and that of da'wah, our marriage will end, but da'wah will always remain rooted in me* . . . I know that it is your right to command me and that it is my duty to obey you, but God in our souls is greater than our souls, *and His da'wah is dearer to us than ourselves* . . .' [emphasis ours]

The horrors of the torture cells where Zainab al-Ghazali and many male and female members of the Muslim Brotherhood were brutally persecuted are so painful to read about, which not only bring tears to the eyes but generate anger and revulsion for Nasir and his administration.

Zainab al-Ghazali's life, sacrifices and achievements have been discussed by both Muslim and non-Muslim writers and continue to be a topic of research in the academic institutions of the world.[1] The present prison memoir has been translated into several languages including Urdu, Bengali and English. The English translation produced from India needed many revisions and improvements. I am glad that my colleague Mokrane Guezzou undertook this task of re-translating the book from the Arabic original and make it accessible to many admirers of Zainab al-Ghazali in the East and the West. I am sure this will be a fascinating and inspiring book to read and will give a fresh insight into the history of the *Ikhwan* and its struggle against a so-called Muslim government bent upon eradicating Islam and foisting upon Egypt a foreign ideology whose demise in recent years in Eastern Europe and the former Soviet Union has been witnessed by the world at large. I am grateful to Miss Susanne Thackray and Mr. Eric R. Fox for the careful editing and reading of the manuscript. We are especially grateful to the author Zainab al-Ghazali for giving us permission to translate and publish this book from the Foundation. May Allah reward all those associated with the production of this book and accept it as a humble contribution to the field of Islamic literature in English.

9 Safar 1415   M. Manazir Ahsan
19 July 1994   Director General

Note

1. Among Western writers on this author, see Valerie J. Hoffman, 'An Islamic Activist: Zaynab al-Ghazali' in Elizabeth W. Fernea (ed.), *Women and the Family in the Middle East: New Voices of Change*, Austin, Texas U.P., 1985; and Miriam Cooke, 'Zaynab al-Ghazali: Saint or Subversive?', *Die Welt des Islams*, Vol. 34, No. 1, April 1994, pp.1-20.

Translator's Introduction

Return of the Pharaoh is the story of a Muslim woman and the torture she was subjected to in the dungeons of Jamal 'Abd al-Nasir, the 'champion of Arab Nationalism', and 'the founder of post-monarchal Egypt'. It is but one story, but it is representative of countless similar stories which have never become known to the general public.

This story relates the efforts of a dedicated Muslim woman and her brothers and sisters in the cause, to make Islam, once again, a living reality, and how they were severely punished for that. In truth, it is the story of a wounded Islam in its own backyard. The story of how Islam had become, and still is, strange and estranged in Egypt and how the callers to Islam were persecuted, imprisoned and killed.

Return of the Pharaoh also tells about the ideological conflict which was, and still is, reigning in Egypt and many other parts of the Muslim world. It tells about the conflicting loyalties that the Muslims, in this case the Egyptian Muslims, face in their lives and in society. On the one hand, the loyalty of the silent majority of Muslims to Islam, traditional values and a way of life they can identify with. This is supported, enhanced and championed by the Islamic movement. And on the other hand, a minority of people uprooted from their origin, alien to the values of their ancestors, and who are, knowingly or unknowingly, serving as tools to safeguard the interests of the wealthy nations.

xi

The severity of such a conflict can only be visualized by the appalling cruelty that Zainab al-Ghazali suffered at the hands of Nasir and his secret police. What happened to her could only happen in a country whose regime is above the law and unaccountable to any authority. Yet, the Muslim world, with rare exceptions, has been ruled, for a long time, by undemocratic regimes having no regard for law and human rights.

The growing tide of Islamic resurgence, usually called Islamic Fundamentalism by Westerners, is an open and growing protest against these undemocratic and selfish regimes.

In order to understand fully the context of the tragedy of Zainab al-Ghazali, one must have an overview of, first, the Muslim Brotherhood (*al-Ikhwan al-Muslimun*) Organization; and second, the political and social conditions during which this important organization was founded.

The Muslim Brotherhood (*Ikhwan*) was founded by Hasan al-Banna (1906-1949) in the Egyptian town of al-Isma'iliyyah in 1928. The son of an Azharite scholar, who earned his livelihood by repairing watches, Hasan al-Banna showed from his early school-days an inclination and great zeal for calling people to Islamic values and traditions. His strong sense of religiosity and spiritual awareness drove him to join the Hasafiyyah *tariqah*, one of many Sufi *tariqahs* that were widespread in Egypt at that time. Even though he was not formally associated with this *tariqah* after he founded the *Ikhwan*, he, nevertheless, maintained a good relation with it, as indeed with other Islamic organizations and religious personalities, and persisted in reciting the litanies (*awrad*, pl. of *wird*) of this *tariqah* until his last days.

Though Hasan al-Banna joined a modern-type school of education, he promised his father that he would continue to memorize the Qur'an, which he did, in fact later, at the age of twelve. While at school, he took part in the activities of some religious associations and clubs which were promoting, and calling for, the observance of Islamic teachings. He also formed, while still at school, an association for the enjoining of good and forbidding of evil.

After finishing school, Hasan al-Banna joined Dar al-Mu'allimin in Damanhur, in 1920, and then went to Dar al-'Ulum in 1923 where he graduated in 1927 as a primary school teacher. He was then assigned to a teaching post in al-Isma'iliyyah.

Hasan al-Banna developed the habit of delivering speeches and organizing study circles in the Mosque near his residence. He used to convey to the people his deep sense of disenchantment with the state of the Muslim *ummah*, and the failure of the religious authorities, in particular al-Azhar University, to redress the status quo. He also expressed doubts about the prevailing political system, and the betrayal by most politicians of the values and principles of the Muslim nation. A group of young workers, who used to attend these speeches and study circles, were so impressed by his comprehensive approach to Islam, his diagnosis of the ills of Muslim society and the cures which he suggested, that they convinced him to form an organization which would take as its mission the revival of Islam. It was a humble beginning, but the speed with which the group grew in the span of just a few years reflected the centuries of Muslims' discontent *vis-à-vis* what was taking place in their society.

The formation of the *Ikhwan* took place four years after the abolition of the Ottoman Caliphate, the last symbol of Muslim strength and dignity. However, the signs of decay and degeneration of Egyptian society appeared centuries before, with Muhammad 'Ali Pasha's reforms, even though the reign of the latter and the subsequent deviations which came with it, were only logical ends to the deviations which preceded his reign.

The formation of the *Ikhwan* was no ordinary event. Had it been so, it would not have stirred Egyptian society, and indeed those of many other Muslim countries, the way it did. There were, at the beginning of this century, and subsequently, scores of Islamic associations, organizations and groups. There existed also different political parties. But the emergence of the *Ikhwan* was an extraordinary event. For out of the ruins of weakness, ideological doubts, still worse perversion to everything Islamic, emerged a group that advocated Islam in its entirety, without apology or complacency. This group was, as Hasan al-Banna pointed out in his *Risalat al-Mu'tamar al-Khamis* (Epistle of the Fifth Congress)[1]: (1) 'a salafi message: for it calls for returning Islam to its pure sources, i.e. The Book of God and the *Sunnah* of His Messenger; (2) a Sunni path: for the *Ikhwan* oblige themselves to following the purified *sunnah* in all their deeds, especially in the domain of beliefs and acts of worship . . .; (3) a Sufi reality: for the *Ikhwan* know that the basis of righteousness is the purification of the soul, transparency of the heart, perseverance in work . . . and love for the sake of God . . .; (4) a political organization: for the *Ikhwan* demand the reform of political order from within and the revision of the relationship of the Muslim *ummah* with other nations . . . as well as teaching people and train them to raise their heads in pride and dignity . . .; (5) a sporting group: for the *Ikhwan* look after their bodies and know that a strong Muslim is better than a weak Muslim . . .; (6) a scientific and cultural league: for Islam makes the seeking of knowledge a religious duty . . .; (7) an economic enterprise: for Islam is interested in the acquiring of money and its use . . .; (8) a social endeavour: for the *Ikhwan* are interested in the ills of society and try to find ways for their cure . . .' This comprehensiveness which Hasan al-Banna had in mind could have passed for a mere theoretical, idealist manifesto similar to countless other manifestos and declarations made by many organizations and religious or political personalities.

But he did, in fact, turn all that he had in mind into a living reality. He surprised Egypt and the Muslim world with his leadership genius, though he was certainly more than a great leader. He left a lasting and positive mark on everyone he met. And this is perhaps why the *Ikhwan* gathered into its fold people with inclinations, interests and backgrounds which would have otherwise appeared impossible to reconcile. The other interesting characteristic about Hasan al-Banna is that he was wholeheartedly involved in what he was doing and he sacrificed everything for what he believed in. He built a strong and sound nucleus of believing men and women on whom the whole Islamic project would stand.

With Hasan al-Banna and the group he founded the bitter rivalry and conflict between the two main religious currents in Egypt at that time, namely the Salafist movement and the Sufi brotherhoods, was resolved once and for all. Al-Azhar, which had a monopoly over Islamic thought through its institutions and networks, was challenged with a new thought which restored to Islam its holistic stature.

In al-Isma'iliyyah, Hasan al-Banna started building the institutions of the *Ikhwan* which included a mosque, general headquarters, Hira' Islamic institution and Umahat al-Mu'minin school for ladies. From these institutions and places of learning the *Ikhwan* message spread to neighbouring cities and villages.

Hasan al-Banna moved, in 1932, to Cairo, and with him the *Ikhwan* headquarters moved too. It was from Cairo that the message of the *Ikhwan* finally spread to the whole of Egypt.

In order that the voice of the *Ikhwan al-Muslimun* should be heard loudly and unequivocally, Hasan al-Banna published two journals, the weekly *al-Ikhwan al-Muslimun* and *al-Nazir* (the Warner). In these journals Hasan al-Banna published some of his small treatises and epistles, though his main concern was not writing books but building good Muslim characters.

As the *Ikhwan* organization became stronger, Hasan al-Banna showed his determination to bring about changes in society. He opened a bureau for community aid and a housing association. He established enterprises of which the most important components were: the Islamic dealings enterprise (*Sharikat al-Mu'amalat al-Islamiyyah*), the Arabic enterprises for mining (*al-Sharika al-Arabiyyah li'l-ma'adin wal'mahajir*), etc. He established hospitals and dispensaries which were controlled and run by the *Ikhwan*. He also organized summer camps for the youth and from these youth he formed scouting groups. He organized international and national outings as well as units for the eradication of illiteracy throughout Egypt. He took a special interest in forming *da'is* and preachers who were sent for teaching and instruction throughout the country. Lastly, the *Ikhwan* were the initiators and promoters of a wave of new books and literature, in terms of their topics and intellectual quality, written by members of the *Ikhwan*.

Parallel to the male organization of the *Ikhwan*, Hasan al-Banna founded a female section (*al-Akhawat al-Muslimat*), to play its role among the ladies. In order to achieve this task the *Akhawat* founded the 'Girls' House for Islamic Education' (*Dar al-Tarbiyyah al-Islamiyyah li'l-fatat*) whose role among ladies and girls was similar to that of the male section in terms of comprehensiveness and depth.

Hasan al-Banna could not ignore what was happening on the political front. Had he ignored it, he would have failed to rise to the wholeness and compass which he set his group to achieve. Had he left politics aside, his group would have had enhanced the claim, already widespread at that time among the intellectuals of Egyptian society, that Islam is a mere personal relationship between man and God, and hence, had nothing to do with political legitimacy.

Soon the *Ikhwan* group made its political voice heard by friend and foe alike. It stood firmly, in the early thirties against the missionary activities which exploited the ignorance, misery and vulnerability of ordinary people and the *Ikhwan* made sure that these activities did not succeed. They also opposed strongly the 1936 Anglo-Egyptian treaty which the Wafdist government signed on behalf of Egypt, for they believed it to be a treaty which strengthened Britain's grip on Egypt.

Hasan al-Banna mobilized all his group's strength and potential to helping the Palestinian people in their 1936 revolution against the British and the Zionists. The voice of the *Ikhwan* was a loud cry against the corruption of the establishment which ruled Egypt at that time. Thus, the *Ikhwan* opposed colonialist and capitalist projects which were implemented in the area through the political system. In this context the *Ikhwan* mobilized the masses to march against the Sidqi-Bevin treaty, in 1946, leading to its failure. This was but a small reaction which was part of an overall plan to get rid of all aspects of colonialism and dependency.

The colonial powers were well aware of the danger posed by the *Ikhwan*, and Hasan al-Banna in particular, to their interests in the region and the threat which they would face should the *Ikhwan* ever get into power. Thus, when Hasan al-Banna presented himself for parliamentary election, the Wafdist Prime Minister, Mustafa al-Nahhas asked him to withdraw his candidature because of threats he had received from the British ambassador in Cairo. Meanwhile the *Ikhwan*'s help for the Palestinian cause did not stop with the end of the 1936 revolution. Hasan al-Banna sent people from his group to train the Palestinians and initiated huge fund-raising schemes for this cause. In the 1948 Arab-Zionist War, the *Ikhwan* sent to the war-front the best of their youth to fight against the Zionists.

Involved as they were in Egyptian affairs, the *Ikhwan* were also keen to expand their thought and vision to other parts of the Muslim world. *Ikhwan* branches, with a close, organizational affiliation with the mother-organization in Egypt, were founded in Syria, Jordan, and later on, in almost all Arab countries. The *Ikhwan* were even involved in the 1948 Yemenite revolution which attempted to enthrone Qadi Abdullah Ibn Ahmad al-Wazir as *Imam* of Yemen after the death of *Imam* Yahya.

Some of the leaders of the Algerian association of Muslim scholars, such as al-Fudail al-Warthilani, had strong links with the *Ikhwan* who were helping them to rid the country of the French colonialists.

Hasan al-Banna's political plans were not simplistic and aimed only at making partisan noises or party political gains. He did not aim, in the long run, at participating in the political game which the dying monarchy, and the colonialist powers, were playing in Egypt. Clearly, he was planning to change Egypt's political system, and hence, overthrow the monarchy, as a first step towards reviving a great Muslim Caliphate.

In order to achieve this aim, he formed an elite core of soldiers, and some civilians, which became known as *al-Jihaz al-Sirri* (the secret organ).

The activities of this secret *Ikhwan* organization among the Egyptian army culminated in the formation of *al-Dubbat al-Ahrar* (the Free Army Officers). This organization included some Egyptian army elite among whom was Jamal 'Abd al-Nasir. Nasir and many of his fellow-officers who participated, later on, in the overthrow of King Faruq did, in fact, belong to the *Ikhwan* and swore allegiance to Hasan al-Banna and the head of the secret organization, Mahmud Labib, whom Hasan al-Banna appointed. Hasan al-Banna did not, however, live to see King Faruq overthrown nor the subsequent turn of events which followed.

After the 1948 Arab-Israeli War, the colonialist powers were convinced that they had to act drastically against the *Ikhwan* and their leader. Thus, all the *Ikhwan* members who participated in the war against the Zionists were imprisoned, and most of the *Ikhwan* members remaining in Egypt were also arrested. But Hasan al-Banna was left free, in order to facilitate his assassination. The great powers were growing ever more concerned about their interests in the region so, because of the *Ikhwan's* activities, the liquidation of its leader and severe measures against the group became inevitable. Hasan al-Banna was assassinated on 12th February 1949.

The key role that Zainab al-Ghazali and Sayyid Qutb played in the history of the *Ikhwan* began to take shape after the death of Hasan al-Banna.

Sayyid Qutb was a renown poet, writer and literary critic. His name was, up to the late thirties, associated with the great writer Abbas Mahmud al-Aqqad. But this association began to fade when Sayyid Qutb's Islamic commitment grew stronger. Before that, however, Sayyid Qutb was a secular writer.

The Islamic awakening in Sayyid Qutb happened quite accidentally. He was writing some books about the linguistic merits of the Qur'an, and for this he studied closely the sacred text of the Qur'an. During the course of this study, Sayyid Qutb strongly and genuinely came to believe that he had found all the answers to the questions which tormented his agitated soul. A series of Islamic books ensued, the most famous and influential being *Social Justice in Islam* (al-'Adala al-Ijtima'iyyah fi'l-Islam). After this period Sayyid Qutb did not write any literary pieces; all his subsequent publications were either political or Islamic.

But if Sayyid Qutb's relations with the Islamic cause began rather late, his political activity started quite early. His father was a member of the Nationalist Party of

Mustafa Kamil. He, himself, was a member of al-Wafd Party, partly because of an uncle's close connection with this party and partly because of al-Aqqad's influence, that is until he resigned in the mid-forties because of his disenchantment with the party.

His incisive and uncompromising articles against the British and the monarchy brought him numerous enemies but also the admiration of the Egyptian people and the respect and veneration of the nationalist and Islamic tendencies. He was a hero in the eyes of many people. The political scene in Egypt during the first half of this century was dominated by corrupt people, apart from a few personalities and the *Ikhwan*. Therefore, the honesty, bravery and political struggle of this great literary figure, Sayyid Qutb, against corruption and foreign dependency was an inspiration and sign of hope for everyone. Sayyid Qutb showed in his attacks against the monarchy and the British that he did not fear death or the loss of his social privileges.

As time passed, the tone of Sayyid Qutb's attacks on the monarchy and the British grew stronger. As a way of silencing his angry voice of discontent, he was sent for two years (1948-50) to the USA to study the educational methodologies of that country.

Up to this time, Sayyid Qutb did not have any formal or informal connections with the *Ikhwan*. Although he was aware of their activities and the efforts made by Hasan al-Banna, it seems that he was not convinced, until his time spent in the United States, that the *Ikhwan* were the effective tool by which Egyptian society could be changed.

Sayyid Qutb was in hospital in the United States when he witnessed the jubilation in many quarters, at the death of Hasan al-Banna. He was told, when he inquired about the reason for this jubilation, that the greatest enemy of the West had been killed. From that moment Sayyid Qutb decided that he would join the *Ikhwan* as soon as he returned to Egypt. He realized that the colonial powers would not consider a person, and his organization, to be their arch-enemy unless that person was a strong and efficient patriot whose activities genuinely threatened the status quo and the colonialists' interests in the area. After all, his vision of a group of people who would emerge out of the ruins of corruption in his native Egypt, and to whom he dedicated his book *Social Justice in Islam*, was not merely a dream but a living reality which he had hitherto failed to notice. Sayyid Qutb saw that the vehicle of change, which he often wished would emerge in his society, was already in motion.

Once in Egypt, Sayyid Qutb rose quickly in the organizational hierarchy of the *Ikhwan*. He was elected, in 1952, as a member of the consultative council (*Maktab al-Irshad*) and head, an influential and important post, of the section for spreading *da'wah* (*qism nashr al-Da'wah*). Later, he was appointed editor of *al-Ikhwan al-Muslimun* journal.

Sayyid Qutb was arrested on Nasir's orders in January 1954 but was released in July 1955, for health reasons. He was again arrested in 1955 and sentenced to 15 years in prison, but was released in 1964 after the intervention of the Iraqi President 'Abd Al-Salam 'Arif. But his freedom lasted only a short time; he was again arrested in 1965 and was sentenced to death for an alleged conspiracy to assassinate Nasir and overthrow his regime. He was executed on 29th August 1966.

As for Zainab al-Ghazali, she was one of the most prominent dignitaries of Egyptian society. Her pious husband was a rich and influential man, with acquaintances and friends from a wide range of political convictions and tendencies. Her own family was politically active and respected by large sections of the Egyptian establishment and opposition alike.

She founded, while still very young, an Islamic women's organization, *Jama'at al-Sayyidat al-Muslimat*, which was very active on the Egyptian social scene. It was this group that

Hasan al-Banna wanted to merge with his women's section, *al-Akhawat al-Muslimat*. Hasan al-Banna wanted Zainab al-Ghazali to be president of *al-Akhawat al-Muslimat*, and make her newly founded group part of the edifice of the *Ikhwan*. This, however, did not come about even though Zainab al-Ghazali swore allegiance to Hasan al-Banna shortly before he was assassinated.

After the death of Hasan al-Banna, Hasan al-Hudaibi was chosen as supreme guide (*al-Murshid al-'Am*) of the *Ikhwan*. This choice was not welcomed by all the *Ikhwan*; some members of the secret organization, backed by others, stormed the general headquarters and occupied it for a while.

However this dissent was contained and the people behind it were expelled from the group. Though the *Ikhwan*, at this stage, did have some very able leaders beside the *Murshid*, nevertheless, the gap which Hasan al-Banna left was clearly felt. Meanwhile the gulf between the *Ikhwan* and Nasir and the government of Free Army Officers was widening. For although the movement of Free Army Officers which overthrew King Faruq was initiated by the *Ikhwan*, the *Ikhwan* became disillusioned at the turn of events after 1952.

When it became clear that Nasir was not going to bring about what the *Ikhwan*, as well as the nationalist and Islamic tendencies, wanted him to achieve, the *Ikhwan* began openly opposing him. Nasir suspended the publication of *al-Ikhwan al-Muslimun*. This was due to the *Ikhwan*'s opposition to the British-Egyptian treaty which Nasir signed in 1954. When Nasir did not succeed in getting his allies, among the secret organization which Hasan al-Banna founded, to take over the leadership of the *Ikhwan*, he saw this open opposition to his policies as a declaration of war against his regime.

He arrested all the *Ikhwan*'s leaders, including the *Murshid* Hasan al-Hudaibi and Sayyid Qutb. After a mock trial, the greatest and most able of the *Ikhwan* leadership were sentenced to death. By this single act, the *Ikhwan* were left practically without effective leadership. Even Hasan al-Hudaibi would not have escaped execution had he not had a heart-attack while awaiting trial. But the greatest of all the losses which the *Ikhwan* suffered at this time was the execution of 'Abd al-Qadir 'Awdah and Shaikh Muhammad Farghali. These two had inherited almost all the qualities of their leader Hasan al-Banna. The loss of these two main figures when the group needed them most was a severe blow which threatened the very existence of the organization.

For the first time since its inception the *Ikhwan* faced a real organizational and leadership crisis. The severe test which the *Ikhwan* was subjected to shook the resolve of many members. Conviction and firm loyalty to the group was not taken for granted as was the case during the lifetime of Hasan al-Banna and prior to the *fitnah* of 1954. Hasan al-Hudaibi, even after his release, was not able personally to firmly assume the task of heading his group, due to his poor health and old age. The drastic turn of events needed immediate and decisive action.

At this juncture came the tripartite role played by Sayyid Qutb, Zainab al-Ghazali and 'Abd al-Fattah Isma'il and the consequent events which led to the appalling cruelty they faced, along with other members of the *Ikhwan*, at the hands of Nasir and his agents.

The leadership of the *Ikhwan*, at that time, decided that the restructuring and reorganization of the group was long overdue. The task of doing this fell, by necessity, on the shoulders of several people. Thus the combination of Sayyid Qutb, Zainab al-Ghazali and 'Abd al-Fattah Isma'il was the best and most effective choice that could have been made by the *Ikhwan* leadership.

'Abd al-Fattah Isma'il, a young, dedicated member of the *Ikhwan*, was considered to be one of the *Ikhwan* youth closest to Hasan al-Banna. But his organizational skills, as was to be proved later on, was perhaps behind his choice for this mission. Zainab al-Ghazali was a social figure who was loved and respected by all strata of society. Her influence within women's sections of society and her family ties and acquaintances, besides her own attributes, opened the way to large and important sections of society. The value of this lady was instantly recognized by 'Abd al-Fattah Isma'il. As for Sayyid Qutb, he was a great intellectual and theoretician. His intellectual and visionary grandeur were endearing aspects which the *Ikhwan* needed desperately. These three persons with their different abilities, importance and tasks, were going to restore to the *Ikhwan* group its past glory and carry out the goals which Hasan al-Banna had set his group to achieve: 'Abd al-Fattah Isma'il and Zainab al-Ghazali from outside and Sayyid Qutb from inside prison, with the guidance and supervision of the supreme guide Hasan al-Hudaibi.

With the passing years, the *Ikhwan*'s strength and effectiveness increased. The growing influence which the thought of the *Ikhwan* exercised on people, especially the youth, attracted enormous attention. Huge numbers of the Egyptian people were recruited and Islamically trained. Study circles, meetings, camps and gatherings were run and directed by the *Ikhwan* throughout the country. Sayyid Qutb's writings especially were read by millions of people both inside and outside Egypt.

The *Ikhwan*, which Nasir thought was dead was emerging, once again, as the biggest political force in Egyptian society. Some official reports indicated that Sayyid Qutb, especially after his release from prison in 1964, was preparing a core of selected *Ikhwan* members to form a 'secret military organization' within the *Ikhwan*. This was enough for Nasir to arrest all the *Ikhwan* members, including Sayyid Qutb, Zainab al-Ghazali and 'Abd al-Fattah Isma'il, and inflict on them the most dreadful cruelty.

These are, in brief, the circumstances which surrounded and explain the political and social context which led to the events related by Zainab al-Ghazali in *Return of the Pharaoh*.

Zainab al-Ghazali is today a renowned Muslim *da'iyah* respected by all Muslim activists. She regularly gives talks and lectures in Egypt and all over the world. She also contributes to many Islamic journals and magazines on Islamic and women's issues.

The hardship and severe tests which Zainab al-Ghazali was subjected to, her firmness and bravery in facing the enemies of Islam, her deep *iman* in God and the Islamic cause, serve as examples for all who strive for the establishment of a state ruled by Divine Law. The story of Zainab al-Ghazali is a story of right against wrong, justice against injustice and dignity against humiliation. The glory of the Muslim *ummah* has faded a little. It is, however, the likes of Zainab al-Ghazali in their firmness and dedication who will restore it, no matter how great the sacrifice.

The events related in this book took place more than a quarter of a century ago. But what is happening today in many parts of the Muslim world is exactly the same as happened to Zainab al-Ghazali and her Muslim brothers and sisters in Islam. For Islamic resurgence has been branded as the West's first enemy by Westerners after the demise of Communism and the disintegration of the Eastern Bloc because of their fear for their interests in the Arab and Muslim regions. In Muslim countries the threat of Islamic resurgence has been used as an excuse by these countries' regimes to hold on to their seats of power.

17 Safar 1415   **Mokrane Guezzou**
27 July 1994

Reference

1. *Majmu'at Rasa'il Hasan al-Banna*. Beirut, second edition, 1981, pp.122-3.

Introduction

*In the Name of Allah, the Merciful, the Compassionate.
Peace and blessings be on our master Muhammad,
his household and Companions.*

Although I have yearned to write *Return of the Pharaoh*,
now for many years, I have, nevertheless, hesitated a
great deal. Had it not been for the many people, whose
belief in the Islamic cause I fully trust, from amongst my
children and brothers, leaders of *da'wah* and exponents of
its thought who lived with me during that period,
believing that it was Islam's right on us that we should
record those days when Islamic *Da'wah* was fought
against, then perhaps it would not have come to fruition.
Those forces of darkness and falsehood, both in the East
and the West, fought hard in those days, against the
Islamic cause. Their objective: to kill off the word of truth
and the people who held its banner. To annihilate all
those activists who believed from the bottom of their
hearts that the Qur'an and the *Sunnah* must be re-
established in society. That the Muslim *Ummah*, be
returned to the land of Islam in order to re-establish a
society of *Tawhid*, knowledge, learning and real
relationship with Allah (may He be exalted). That ungodly
societies, which blinded humanity from its straight path
and God's way, be abolished. For Allah's way is the right
way, and the earth had to be cleansed of the worship of
earthly gods and despots, and the supremacy of *Shari'ah*
had to be established. Once this was achieved, life could
then return to the way Allah wanted it to be, exactly as

1

during the time of the Prophet Muhammad (peace be upon him) and the rule of his blessed Companions.

There is no salvation for this *Ummah* or the world except through calling to Islam. The dungeons of prisons, the instruments of torture and the pains of those so oppressed have but increased the strength, firmness and patience of Muslim activists and thinkers who stood in the face of falsehood. The way to truth is one. It is the way of Allah, His Prophets and Messengers and all their inheritors. As for falsehood, its ways are diverse and many, and on each of these ways there is a devil who embellishes, for those who are absorbed by falsehood, evil deeds and leads people ever more readily towards them. *'Verily, this is My Way, leading straight: follow it, follow not (other) paths, they will scatter you about from His (great) Path . . . .'*[1]

The crucial matter for Muslims is that we are firm in following Allah's way, with full trust in the correctness of our steps and in the clarity of our vision. *'You are the best of people, evolved for mankind . . .'*[2] as well as the signs of establishing complete submission to 'there is no god but Allah and Muhammad is His Messenger'. All that matters to us is adding new bricks to our building. That we do not neglect or retreat from our belief: the belief of *Tawhid*, of work and exposition. An exposition of truth, for all mankind.

We believe that the period of our incarceration and torture is history's right to know of, such that those who are on the way can study and understand it, can remain firm in their conviction and not transform their cause into some kind of sophism, sophistry into opulent talk and mere historical storying. It is for all this that I consented, with the support of the sincere from amongst my children and brothers, to seek Allah's help in collecting together that which my memory still holds.

I hope that Allah will help me to recollect what happened, or at least some of it, and that these writings

2

will be a torch of truth, light and guidance for all those who are sincere. Let us plough along a straight path for 'Ours is the message of Prophets and Messengers. Muhammad's message (peace be upon him) is complete and has supremacy. It is through *Shari'ah* that Allah has completed His injunctions and abrogated what preceded it, making it a pure truth "*. . . let him who will, believe, and let him who will, reject (it) . . .*" '3

Those who have assumed the difficulties of this way and know - God willing - the secret behind the teachings of the Qur'an and the *Sunnah* will never deviate from truth, good deeds and *da'wah* until the *Ummah* is re-established and all humanity is under the banner of Allah. We carry on the way of Allah, expecting His reward for whatever we endure, '*Allah has purchased of the believers their persons and their goods; for theirs (in return) is the garden (of Paradise): they fight in His Cause, and slay and are slain: a promise binding on Him in truth, through the law, the Gospel and the Qur'an . . .*'4

This book is for all those martyrs who have gone before us, a token of our love, gratitude and promise that we are still on the way. It is also for all those who have a grain of goodness in them, in the hope that Allah makes them benefit, and guides them, '*But you will not, except as Allah wills . . .*'5

Zainab al-Ghazali al-Jubaili

References

1. *Al-An'am*: 153.

2. *Al 'Imran*: 110.

3. *Al-Kahf*: 29.

4. *At-Tawbah*: 111.

5. *Al-Insan*: 30.

CHAPTER 1

Jamal 'Abd al-Nasir:[1]
Hatred and Vengeance

On my way home one afternoon, on a wintry day in early February 1964, my car suddenly turned upside down after colliding with another vehicle. The sheer force of the collision sent me into a state of semi-consciousness, and despite the severity of my pains the only thing I could comprehend, from all that was happening around me, was the panicky voice of someone calling my name. I can only assume that I then passed out for when I woke up I found myself in Heliopolise Hospital surrounded by my husband, brothers, sisters and some of my colleagues in *da'wah*. As was evident from the expression on their faces they were all acutely distressed but within seconds I passed out again.

I can recall mumbling: 'Thank God, thank God!', as if enquiring about what happened. It then all came flooding back, and I could hear my husband's relief as he said: 'Praise be to Allah, He has saved her. Thank Allah *Hajjah*.'[2]

I enquired about my driver who, I was told, was well - praise be to Allah - and receiving treatment in hospital. I found out later that he was suffering from cerebral concussion. As for myself, I was taken to the X-ray room where it was established that my thigh bone was broken. As a temporary measure my leg was placed in an iron

5

cage ready for my transferral to Mazhar 'Ashur Mustafa Hospital, where surgeon Muhammad Abdullah was to operate on me. The operation itself took three and a half hours and even then my condition remained critical for some time. Once I did begin to recover it did not take me long to establish both from what I overheard and what was reported to me that the accident was no accident at all. It had been planned by Nasir's secret agents, with the express intent to kill me.

Up until these events, a group of Muslim youth used to visit me on a daily basis. First among them was Brother 'Abd al-Fattah Isma'il. Clearly now with Nasir's ambitions for me, I could no longer allow these visits to continue and therefore informed my respected brother of my decision. He informed me that he had already requested just that of the youth but they were insistent that nothing should change. Their visits would go ahead as usual.

On another occasion, the Muslim Ladies Group's administrative secretary tried to give me a file which she wanted to show me in my capacity as President of this group. Both my husband and the wife of Hasan al-Hudaibi, the supreme guide (al-Murshid al-'Am) of the Muslim Brotherhood[3] (al-Ikhwan al-Muslimun) were in my room at this time. I watched helplessly as my husband quickly guided my visitor away and I overheard him reminding the secretary that he had already forbidden her giving me any work-related documents. My husband's explanation, when I tried to find out what was going on, was that Doctor Abdullah's permission was necessary before I undertook any kind of activity. The doctor later, and after an examination of my leg, confirmed that it was he who had ordered that none of the group's documents or news should reach me. I protested, claiming that it was a simple matter of signing a few documents, but he was adamant. The days passed by slowly and again I begged the doctor to allow me to do some of the group's work. My requests were met with the same refusal. By now though I was certain that there was something which everyone was trying to hide from me.

In what seemed like weeks later, and after mustering great courage, the secretary again came to inform me, in the presence of my husband, of the decree to close down the General Headquarters of the Muslim Ladies Group. I could hardly believe my ears and almost snatched the papers from her only to read its confirmation in black and white.

'*Alhamdu Lillah*, but the government has no right to do this, we are an Islamic group.'

'No one can say to this government it has no right. We have tried everything, but Nasir is adamant about dissolving the group. Worse still, he hates you personally, *Hajjah* Zainab! for he can't stand the mentioning of your name in his presence. If anybody does make reference to you he immediately stops the meeting with whoever has done so.'

'Praise be to Allah that he fears me and detests me. I too detest him, for Allah. Nasir's despotism only serves to increase our persistence to please our consciences and live for the fulfilment of our mission, the mission of *tawhid*. We will triumph, *insha' Allah*, and the least that we can give for that is to be martyred for its sake.'

'*Hajjah*', she said with tears in her eyes, 'the matter is very serious, I pray also to Allah that it won't end with the banning of our Group. But perhaps the very words you say now are being recorded, they may have bugged the room.'

The secretary whispered these words into my ear as if she were afraid that what she said was true, and she carried on whispering: '*Hajjah*, I request you to do a small thing, please sign this paper. If you do, the decree to ban our group will be reversed.'

I asked her to hand over the piece of paper. It was a membership card for the Socialist Union.

'No, by Allah. May my hand be paralysed if I ever sign that which will incriminate me, in front of Allah, with acquiescing to the despotic rule of Nasir who killed 'Abd al-Qadir 'Awdah and his colleagues. Those who have soiled their hands with the blood of the faithful, are adversaries of Allah and of all believers. It is more honourable for us to let the Muslim Ladies Group be dissolved.'

She kissed my head, and with tears in her eyes, asked: 'Do you trust that I am your daughter?'

'Yes!'

'Then leave this issue.'

'We will leave it, and I won't sign this paper. Our signature implies allegiance to a despot, which is an impossible thing for us to do. Allah will do that which He chooses for His Servants.'

Several more days passed in hospital, and then to my relief it was decided that I could continue the treatment at home.

Dealings with the Socialist Union

At home, the secretary would visit me daily, and on one occasion quite out of the blue she informed me that the ban decree had been lifted. Surprised, I asked how this had happened.

'I honestly don't know, but it may well be for the sake of opening up channels of communication with you.'

Despite a return visit to the hospital for an operation to remove the pins from my thigh, I had by now assumed my function of running the affairs of the Muslim Ladies Group from home. Meanwhile, *(Imam Shahid)* Sayyid Qutb had been released and together with a number of Muslim brothers, visited me in hospital. Imagine my surprise

8

then when a recorded delivery item arrived containing a
card with the inscription:

'Arab Socialist Union'
Liberty-Socialism-Unity

Name: Zainab al-Ghazali al-Jubaili, known as:
Zainab al-Ghazali.
Occupation: President of The Muslim Ladies
Group.
Borough: al-Basatin-Almaza.
County: Misr al-Jadidah.
District: al-Qahirah.

Enclosed with the card was a receipt showing that my
membership fee for 1964 had been paid. I laughed bitterly
at what had become of Egypt; we used to live in freedom,
but the military *coup* had changed all that.[4] Thereafter,
invitations from the Socialist Union, to attend its meetings,
began pouring through my letter-box. I ignored them.
Instead my energies were concentrated on gradually
resuming my activities in the general office of the Muslim
Ladies Group; with the aid of a walking stick my
movements were now less inhibited.

I was in the general office one morning when the
phone rang; the secretary wanted me to speak with
someone from the Socialist Union. I picked up the phone:
'Assalam Alaikum.'

'Wa Alaikum assalam.'

'Yes, what can I do for you?'

The caller asked me if I was Zainab al-Ghazali, and
when my answer was in the affirmative he said: 'This is
the Socialist Union. The members of the Muslim Ladies'
administrative committee, and you first and foremost,

are requested to take your banners and go to the airport to welcome the President home.'

'*Insha' Allah*, Allah does what He wills and chooses.'

'This is our request, we want the administrative committee, as well as a great number of the general committee's members to be present. If you require, we will arrange for a car to be at your disposal.'

'Thank you.'

Here the call ended.

A few days later, I received another phone call from the Socialist Union. It was a lady; she wanted to know why we had not been present at the airport to welcome the President. By way of response I said: 'We members of the Muslim Ladies' administrative committee, and the general council, all observe Islamic behaviour, therefore, we cannot be present in such crowded welcomes.'

'How can that be Madam Zainab? It seems that you don't want to co-operate with us. Did you inform the other members and did they each in turn refuse?'

'How could I have informed them when I am not convinced of your request which runs counter to the teachings of Islam?'

'You are not co-operating with us!'

'We stick to the teachings of the Qur'an and the *Sunnah*. Our pact is with Allah, our co-operation can only be in issues of good and beneficence. Perhaps you will concede that the telephone is not a suitable medium for such a discussion?'

'You are welcome here! We will wait for you in the Socialist Union's Headquarters in 'Abidin Square to discuss this issue.'

'Unfortunately, I am sick, and my movements limited because of a serious injury to my leg. If you please you are welcome in the Muslim Ladies Headquarters.'

'Come to see us on your way home, are you not a member of the Socialist Union?'

'I am a member of the Muslim Ladies Group, *assalamu alaiki*, my daughter, *wa rahmatu Allah*!'

I ended the call, and did not go to see her.

A week later our group secretary showed me a recorded letter dated 15th September 1964, containing Ministerial Decree No. 32 dated 6th September 1964, which informed us once again of the Government's decision to ban the Muslim Ladies Group.

'NO' to the Despot!

The Muslim Ladies Group's administrative committee held an urgent meeting that same day. The committee rejected both the dissolution decree and the hand over of its property and belongings to another group whose members, although part of our group, had been separated from us at the instigations of the Secret Services before Nasir's *coup*. After the *coup* this group had become Nasir's tool. Our administrative committee had also decided to call our general council to an urgent meeting, within the next 24 hours. Here, too, the general committee rejected the dissolution of our Group and agreed to refer the case to the courts.

We recruited a lawyer, Dr. Abdullah Rashwan, to defend our case. Meanwhile, we sent recorded letters and messages to the Presidency, the Home Office, the Ministry of Social Affairs and the Attorney General, along with duplicate copies to the press, informing all these parties that the Muslim Ladies Group was established in 1936 for the promotion of Islamic *da'wah* and the return of Muslims to their Lord's Book and the *Sunnah* of His Messenger. Hence, neither the Home Office nor the Ministry of Social Affairs had any bond of allegiance from our group. For allegiance is, after all, due only to Allah and to those who establish His religion and laws. Our letter read:

11

The Muslim Ladies Group was established in 1936 to spread the message of Allah and to strive for the making of a Muslim *Ummah* which will bring back to Islam its glory and own state. Our group works for the sake of Allah, and no secular government has the right of sovereignty over Muslims.

The Muslim Ladies Group's message is a call to Islam. It recruits men, women, the young and the old, in order that they believe in Allah's message and establish a state that takes what He revealed as its law.

We, the Muslim Ladies, reject the ban decree on our Group, for the President, who is openly calling for the secularization of the state, has no right of allegiance from us. Neither has the Ministry of Social Affairs any right of allegiance from us; *Da'wah* represents neither money nor belongings which can be confiscated by a secular state whose members are fighting Allah, His Messenger and the Muslim *Ummah*.

Let the state confiscate our money and belongings, but it cannot confiscate our faith. Our message is one of *da'wah* and of people who perform this *da'wah*. We stand underneath the umbrella of 'there is no god but Allah and Muhammad is His Messenger'. Belief in this formula compels us to strive continuously for the establishment of an Islamic state by a community that is conscientious of its religion, is governed by Allah's law, and is always striving in His cause.

Firm in his resolve to eliminate our Group, Nasir issued a military decree preventing publication of our magazine for an unlimited period. The despot's agents even invaded our Headquarters and removed all the contents. As a result, they displaced 120 orphans whose needs, in terms of shelter and education, from nursery to university level, had been taken care of by the Group.

It is only right that I should proudly record here, that the despot's agents did not find a single lady, from amongst either the general council or administrative committee or the preachers' board, waiting to hand them the keys of our Headquarters. Nasir's agents had asked me to hand over the keys to them personally but I refused as did all our other members. Finally the keys were secured from the administrative secretary, but then, as an employee, that person had no choice.

What Next?

Before long, members of the Muslim Ladies Group began flocking to my house asking me what we should do.

Dear reader! The stance which the Muslim Ladies took, it should be recalled, was in 1964, when Nasir's rule was at its zenith. At a time when many people preferred to conceal what they really thought. Such people used to endorse the despot's actions, and even worse some issued *Fatwas* in support of Nasir's deeds. They would ascribe to Nasir things which made a demigod of him. Believing something and displaying exactly the opposite (*taqiyyah*),[5] while discrediting those who refuse to do the same, is not something Islam ascribes to. A true Muslim does not waste his or her own faith nor is the mocking of Muslim brothers and sisters permitted. Yet many supposed Islamic magazines competed to please the despot. Even *al-Azhar* magazine, which was once dear to our hearts, opened its pages to hypocritical writers who competed to please falsehood and its folk. *Fatwas* which defamed the *Mujahids* who opted for *'azimah* and shunned the error they called *rukhsah*,[6] began pouring from some government-employed

13

scholars. They hurled abuse at those *Mujahids* who called people to practise Islam and not merely belong to it by name; for Islam is practise, not lip-service.

The Muslim Ladies Group neither refused to follow what some people called *rukhsah*, nor did it stop short of belonging to Islam. Instead, the Muslim Ladies raised the banner of truth and pronounced the word of truthfulness, at a time when a great many people denounced them for fear of losing their jobs, their careers and their homes. The Muslim Ladies did not stand by as spectators, but spoke frankly about the events which were going on, seeking Allah's pleasure, even if in the process it upset many people. The members of our Group continued to meet and as for myself I had dedicated my whole life to the Muslim Ladies; it was my *raison d'etre*. For I had pledged to Allah on the day I established the Group that I would never submit my life to anybody beside Him. The huge number of Muslim ladies who poured into my house renewed their pledge to dedicate their lives to following Allah's way and to calling people to it. They agreed with me to hold meetings in their homes whereby our preachers would teach the ladies the principles of Islam. But sadly our opportunities were few for the despot's state machine was watching anyone who called to Allah in these kind of meetings. One by one the ladies who held these meetings were contacted by Nasir's agents and threatened. In this way the state obtained an undertaking, from all the ladies involved, that they would not hold such meetings again. Thereafter our activities were confined to those of a personal nature.

Bargaining and Deception

Nasir's security and police agents renewed their contacts with me. They wanted to meet in order to present their offers to me; the implication being that I should buy this world for the Next. For instance, they suggested the re-publication of the Muslim Ladies' magazine, with me as its Editor-in-Chief with a salary of E£300 per month; in return I was to have nothing to do with what was to be written in the magazine. Naturally, I refused. It would have been unthinkable for the Muslim Ladies' magazine to be issued from the Security Forces' Headquarters let alone assist in the spread of secularization. They also offered to cancel the ban decree on our Group and to give us back our Headquarters with an annual support fund totalling E£20,000; in return we had to form one of the Socialist Union institutions. Again I refused, advising the despot's agents that our activities will, *insha' Allah*, be only for the sake of Allah. The Muslim Ladies Group was not ready to deceive or mis-represent anything. For those who gain their earnings under the pretext of working for Islam cannot really serve it.

My rebuttals obviously angered them but still they persisted in their ridiculous temptations. Before long the truth behind their sinister offers would become apparent.

The Night Predators

At home one evening, three men knocked on the door and asked permission to come in. I found them in the living room and immediately noticed that they were wearing head-dress. After greeting them, they introduced themselves as Syrians travelling from Saudi Arabia to visit Egypt for a few days. They also told me that they had met, in Saudi Arabia, Sa'id Ramadan, Shaikh Mustafa al-'Alim, Kamil al-Sharif, Muhammad al-'Ashmawi and Fathi al-Khuli (all of them members of the *Ikhwan* who had fled from Nasir and his despotism). They explained that the same had requested them to convey *salam* to the *Ikhwan* of Egypt and would welcome assurances that

15

both members of the *Ikhwan* here and 'the organization', are all well. The same visitors also reported that Sa'id Ramadan, and company, had asked them to join the organization, and that they were ready to execute orders and stay in Egypt to help the *Ikhwan*.

They talked about the *Ikhwan* and Nasir and how the latter persisted in persecuting the former. They spoke about the 1954 events, the dissolution of the *Ikhwan* and the execution of 'Abd al-Qadir 'Awdah and his friends. The time was right and they were ready - so they claimed - to take revenge and kill Nasir. This decision, they continued, was also the opinion held by Kamil al-Sharif, al-'Ashmawi, al-Khuli and al-'Alim.

As I was only listening to them and did not respond they openly asked my opinion: 'You speak of things and names about which I know nothing', I replied.

'Sister Zainab, we will come back again to know the *Murshid*'s and the organization's opinion about what we have said to you.'

I responded briefly: 'First, I do not know anything called "the organization" in the *Ikhwan* group, for as far as I am aware the *Ikhwan* were dissolved by the State. Second, I do not speak with the *Murshid* concerning these issues, for our friendship and relationship with him is but Islamic brotherhood and familial love. Third, in my understanding, killing Nasir has never been considered by the *Ikhwan*. Therefore, I advise you to go back to your country and to train yourselves Islamically.'

'It seems', responded one of them, 'that sister Zainab is not convinced. Who destroyed the country if not Nasir?'

'In my understanding it is not the *Ikhwan*'s message to kill Nasir.'

I then asked them to give me their names. Stutteringly, one of them told me that they were: 'Abd al-Shafi 'Abd al-Haq, 'Abd al-Jalil 'Isa and 'Abd al-Rahman Khalil. I laughed to myself for the simple reason that all their names were preceded by 'Abd and furthermore that only one person delivered the advice.

Once again I cautioned them: 'Go back to your country before Nasir's security agents catch up with you, that is if you do not know them already and have nothing to do with them, which I very much doubt.'

The retort was clear.

'You're right to be suspicious of us. We'll visit you again soon and then you'll know who we are.'

With that they left.

When Brother 'Abd al-Fattah Isma'il visited me, sometime after this incident, I related to him the story of these so-called Syrian visitors.

The Many Faces of Ahmad Rasikh

Less than two weeks after the Syrians' visit, I was, much to my surprise, called upon by another man who identified himself as Ahmad Rasikh, and as a security agent. He asked me about the content of my conversation with the Syrians. I explained that I was well aware that those men were spies sent by the security forces. I made it a point to tell him that this kind of behaviour was childish, for what else did the security forces want from me after confiscating our Group's Headquarters and banning our magazine?

He responded with the most bizarre questions, asking me what I had meant by Jamalov and Jamalovs[7] in my conversation with the Syrians.

'Those are atheists, who are proud of belonging to falsehood and its high-priests.'

He quickly changed the subject: '*Hajjah*, we are Muslims!'

'Muslims are different (They say: *Our hearts are concealed from that which you invite us to, and in our ears is a deafness and between us and you is a screen: so you do what you will*).'[8]

'You will be Minister of Social Affairs from tomorrow if you agree to our demands.'

I made no attempt to conceal my sarcasm: 'True Muslims are not tempted by mere position, and do not participate in atheist, secular governments. As for the position of the Muslim lady, it will be decided by the Islamic State whenever it is established. Now what do you want from me?'

'We want an agreement with you.'

'This is impossible! An agreement cannot be struck between people who call for disbelief and raise the banner of falsehood, and people who call for the *Tawhid* of Allah and belief in Him alone. Repent to Allah and ask for His forgiveness. I would like to bring this meeting to an end please!'

The man calling himself Ahmad Rasikh had in any case already finished drinking his coffee and now stood up to leave, saying: 'By Allah, we only want to reach an agreement with you. And when we do, it will be you who issues the decree lifting the ban on the Muslim Ladies Group and its magazine.'

'Thank you, but Islam can do without groups and organizations which agree to be agents of Allah's enemies. May Allah guide you and forgive you.'

Two days later, as I was sitting on the balcony, a car stopped in front of my door, and a man wearing dark clothes got out.

'*Assalamu alaikum Hajjah* Zainab!'

I returned his greeting and asked him to come inside the house. He came through to the guest-room and introduced himself as Ahmad Rasikh from the security forces. I could not help gazing at him, as if I was measuring his length and width, for not only had I once been to the Secret Police's offices to meet a person called Ahmad Rasikh but when I went to see this man, there was a pad on his desk which had the same name, Ahmad

18

Rasikh, written on it. What was more this new Ahmad Rasikh talked with me about the person who had visited me only two days earlier. As you will recall, dear reader, this man also happened to be called Ahmad Rasikh. One name for three men and all wishing to talk with me!

My astonishment was impossible to conceal and as I explored the man's features he asked: 'Are you surprised that I have come to visit you, *Hajjah* Zainab?'

My response deliberately aimed to mock: 'I am surprised for something quite different. This house always welcomes, with magnanimity, both expected and unexpected guests. However I will relate to you a story that I read in *al-Ahram*,[9] if I can remember it correctly: Two hundred years ago, the King and Queen of Holland went to England following an invitation from the monarchs of that country. The King of England's attention was drawn to the interest which the Queen of Holland showed in a dog running around the reception hall. For the Queen of Holland had rushed to this dog and grabbed it, holding and kissing it passionately and fervently, as if she had lost her mind. She, then, handed it over to her husband, while whispering something into his ear and pointing to the dog's eyes. The King of Holland, in turn, began kissing the dog. Naturally, their hosts were curious but nevertheless said nothing. Then, the Queen of Holland took the dog from her husband, while wiping away her tears, and held it against her chest as if it were her own dear child. When the Royal couple were taken for dinner, the Queen took the dog with her and fed it herself. The Queen of England mentioned in passing that the dog belonged to her daughter but the King, wanting to know the secret behind his guests' attachment to this dog concluded, as if by apology: 'Had my daughter not been so attached to this dog, I would gladly give it to you.' Then, the Queen of Holland, who believed in re-incarnation, informed her hosts that she had a deceased son whose spirit was incarnated in this dog, and that the dog's eyes matched exactly those of her son's. The King of England, thereafter, persuaded his daughter, who was also present, to make a gift of the dog to his guests.

'Mr. Rasikh, people who believe in incarnation claim some resemblance between the deceased person and the form in which it is incarnated. However, now, within a relatively short span of time, I have met with three men, each calling themselves Ahmad Rasikh, but none of you look alike, neither in height and skin-colour nor in looks. Has your President then decided to profess a new school of incarnation and asked you to follow it?'

The man looked at me in bewilderment: 'I am truly Ahmad Rasikh, we are good people *Hajjah* Zainab, and we want to reach an agreement with you.'

'This has no importance', I retorted. 'What do you want?'

'The government is very keen to reach an agreement with you. We know that the *Ikhwan* deceived you and convinced you to follow their principles. It was thanks to the *Ikhwan* that your group was banned and your Headquarters confiscated. The *Ikhwan* are trouble-makers. We would like you to agree with us, for what we want to know is very simple: the names of all the active members of the *Ikhwan*. By Allah, *Hajjah*, the President will be grateful for this service, and you will see the evidence of this gratefulness in the next few days. You are a good lady, may Allah prolong your life, and do not have anything to do with the *Ikhwan*'s troubles. It is enough what they have already caused for you with the state.'

The man went on to say that *Imam* al-Hudaibi and *Imam* Sayyid Qutb were doing their best to reach an agreement with the President, but that the President refused to collaborate with them because he did not trust them.

'If you knew', the man said, 'what the *Ikhwan* say about you, you would agree with us and leave these people who are the cause of all the persecution which has happened to you and the Muslim Ladies Group.'

I laughed: 'I will speak with you as a man from the Security Forces, and I care neither about your name nor your shape. First, I believe that even ordinary Muslims know and believe that you are far from Islam. Instead you are doing your best to fight it. Do you want to reach an agreement with truth while you are following falsehood? You import ideologies from both the East and the West. Sometimes you raise the banner of Communism, and at other times you revere the capitalist goddess, lost between the two. It is from within this loss that you derive your legislations and laws. I hope I am frank with you and that my words do not need further interpretation. Islam is other than that which you want.'

'I swear by Allah, *Hajjah*, that I pray the Friday prayer.'

'What about the rest of your obligations?'

'I am used to praying on Friday because my father used to do so and took me with him to the Mosque to perform it.'

'Did you not ask your father why he only prayed on a Friday?'

'Our hearts are Muslim, as long as we say, "there is no god but Allah". It's enough.'

'Without practising the formula "there is no god but Allah" you will find it will be held as an argument against you, not for you, in front of Allah.'

'People follow the religion of their Kings.'

'May He raise them, on the Day of Judgement, with their Kings!'

'I am trying to reach an agreement with you.'

'*Throughout history, never have the apostles' messages met with falsehood. For the people who believed in it submitted to Allah, saying: Our Lord! In You do we trust, and to You do we turn in repentance: to You is our final goal. Our Lord! Make us not a test nor a trial for the unbelievers, but forgive us, our Lord! For You are the Exalted in Might, the Wise.'*[10]

He stood up to leave, saying angrily: 'I will not be coming to see you again. However, if you want to contact me, here is my phone number.'

'Thank you, I do not want it.'

Towards the end of July 1965, I was informed that several *Ikhwan* members had been arrested.

Notes and References

1. Jamal 'Abd al-Nasir (subsequently Nasir) (1918-1970), Egyptian President. Champion of Arab Nationalism and one of the most influential Arab leaders of modern times.

2. *Hajjah* (masc. *Haj*) is a title given to the person who has performed *Hajj*, but is also used as a title of respect, especially for elders.

3. The Muslim Brotherhood (*al-Ikhwan al-Muslimun*) (subsequently *Ikhwan*), was one of the largest and most organized Islamic revivalist movements in the Islamic world. Founded by Hasan al-Banna (1906-1949), in 1928, the *Ikhwan* played a crucial role in shaping the modern political history of Egypt and some other Arab countries.

4. In 1952 a military *coup* changed Egypt from a monarchy into a Republic.

5. *Taqiyyah*: (from the root *waqa* = to safeguard, self-protection and hence dissimulation (in order to protect oneself)). The principle of concealment of one's religious beliefs in order to avoid prosecution or imminent harm. Cf. *The Concise Encyclopaedia of Islam*, Cyril Glace.

6. *'Azimah* (plu. *'Aza'im*) lit. determination, resolution, fixed purpose; in Islam an ordinance as interpreted strictly. Correlative to it is *rukhsah* (plu. *rukhas*) exemption given by the lawgiver for certain cases of prevention or complete dispensation from observance of the law. Cf. *The Encyclopaedia of Islam*, 1st edition.

7. This is, of course, an allusion to Nasir's Soviet-Socialist orientation. In fact, Nasir was, sometimes, more Soviet than the Soviets themselves. This is why the name Jamalov, following the pattern of most Russian names, befitted him. As for the Jamalovs, they are all those who follow in Nasir's footsteps.

8. *Fussilat*: 1.

9. Egypt's largest-selling, State controlled newspaper.

10. *Al-Mumtahanah*: 4 and 5.

CHAPTER 2

The Pledge of Allegiance

My relationship with the *Ikhwan* group was not as recent as some would have it. For it went back to 1937. I met with *Imam Shahid* Hasan al-Banna, for the first time, in those remote blessed days of 1937, six months after I formed the Muslim Ladies Group. The meeting took place in the *Ikhwan's* headquarters, then in al-'Atabah, after I delivered a lecture to the group's ladies' branch.

Hasan al-Banna was in the process of forming a sisters' branch in the *Ikhwan*. After reminding me of the necessity of uniting all Muslims and bringing them together, he invited me to preside over the Muslim sisters. This meant the merging of my new-born Muslim Ladies Group, something I was intensely proud of, with the *Ikhwan*. I promised to discuss al-Banna's suggestion with our general assembly but said I could not give a guarantee about the result. As it happened, our general assembly rejected the proposal but recommended close co-operation between the two groups.

Thereafter, I met with al-Banna repeatedly and even though each of us maintained our own opinions, our Islamic relationship in no way suffered. At the last meeting which took place between us in the Muslim Ladies Headquarters, I sought to appease him by promising to make the Muslim Ladies Group one of the *Ikhwan's*

25

foundation stones, but on condition that we retained our name and independence for the benefit of *da'wah*. Unable to compromise, al-Banna insisted on a complete merger.

Events moved fast after that, and soon we were dealing with the incidents of 1948.[1] A decree was issued to dissolve the *Ikhwan* group, close down all its branches and confiscate its belongings. Before long, thousands of its members were in jail. The Muslim Sisters (the *Ikhwan*'s ladies' branch) had been performing activities they are to be thanked for. One of these sisters was Mrs. Tahiah al-Jubaili, my brother's wife and cousin, and it was from her that I learned many details. It was then, that I found myself, for the first time, eager to support all of al-Banna's opinions and understood his insistence on completely merging the Muslim Ladies Group into the *Ikhwan*. In my office, the same office where my last meeting with al-Banna had taken place, the morning after the dissolution of the *Ikhwan*, I could not help putting my head in my hands and crying bitterly. I believed that al-Banna was right. He was the *Imam* that all Muslims must pledge allegiance to, in order that they struggle for the return of Muslims to their position of responsibility and true existence, and can implement Allah's commands. I felt that al-Banna was stronger than me and franker in disseminating and announcing the truth. His boldness and courage are two characteristics which all Muslims must have. I asked my secretary to contact Brother 'Abd al-Hafiz al-Saifi whom I wanted to convey a verbal message to al-Banna, reminding him of my pledge to him at our last meeting. When al-Saifi returned with al-Banna's greetings and prayers, I requested my brother Muhammad al-Ghazali al-Jubaili to take, or ask his wife to take, a note to al-Banna. That short note read:

Sayyidi[2] *Imam* Hasan al-Banna,

Zainab al-Ghazali presents herself today devoid of everything except her servitude to Allah and her

26

enslavement in the call to Him. You are today the only person who can do to this *Ummah* something for the Call to Allah in a way that pleases Him.

Waiting for your instructions and orders.

Shortly afterwards, my brother informed me that a brief appointment in the Muslim Youth[3] (*al-Shubban al-Muslimun*) Headquarters between myself and al-Banna had been arranged. We were to make out that this meeting took place purely by coincidence. In any case, I was not short of excuses to visit the establishment, for I was about to deliver a lecture there. As arranged, al-Banna and I bumped into each other whilst using the stairs at the Headquarters. Candidly, and without hesitation, I volunteered: 'I pledge allegiance to you for the establishment of the Islamic State. The least I can give for this, is shedding my blood and merging the Muslim Ladies Group with the *Ikhwan*.'

'I accept the pledge, but the Muslim Ladies Group remains as it is.'

We left each other with an agreement that further contact would be made via my brother's house.

The first thing al-Banna charged me to do was to mediate between al-Nahhas and the *Ikhwan*. Mustafa al-Nahhas[4] who was, then, out of office, designated the late Amin Khalil as the person in charge of clearing up the misunderstanding between the two parties. Al-Banna consented, and I was to be the contact.

One evening in February 1949, an agitated Amin Khalil banged on our door and hurriedly explained that he needed me to arrange urgently for al-Banna to leave the country. If he did not then the chances were he would be killed. I immediately set about this task and was about to convey arrangements via my brother when I learned of his arrest as well. I had no choice but to contact al-Banna personally. However I was too late; I was informed that the *Imam* had been shot and taken to hospital. Even worse, his condition was deteriorating. Finally, we heard that his soul had joined the Messengers, the truthful and the martyrs. Whilst my awe was immense, my anger and bitterness towards his murderers was overwhelming and I made no attempt to hide it.

Soon after, a Coalition Government came into power, and issued a ban decree on the Muslim Ladies Group. With the help of 'Abd al-Fattah Hasan, a lawyer, we successfully contested this ban in court and in 1950, during Husain Sirri's[5] term of office, we were able to resume our activities. A Wafd Government followed and the *Ikhwan* resumed its activities under the leadership of *al-Murshid* Hasan al-Hudaibi. I wished to declare my allegiance, but only indirectly until the time was ripe to openly declare it. To this end, I gave my dearest piece of furniture - a large arabesque suite - towards the furnishing of the *Murshid*'s office.

Calm and quiet resumed and, before long, 'Abd al-Qadir 'Awdah visited me to thank me for my gift: 'We are pleased that Zainab al-Ghazali al-Jubaili has joined the *Ikhwan*.'

'I hope to be one of you, God willing.'

'You are already, *alhamdu lillah*.'

My relationship with most of the *Ikhwan* members was amicable and friendly until the military *coup* led by Major General Muhammad Najib.[6] The latter had visited me only days before the *coup*, accompanied by Prince 'Abd Allah al-Faisal, Lais Siraj al-Din, Shaykh al-Baquri[7] and my brother 'Ali al-Ghazali, on the occasion of the Prince's visit to Egypt. In the beginning, both the *Ikhwan* and the Muslim Ladies Group supported the *coup*. However, I soon felt that things had not gone the way we had hoped, and that this was not the revolution to culminate the previous efforts of all those who had tried to save the country. I began to convey my views to all Muslim brothers I met, and when some ministerial posts were offered to the *Ikhwan*, I stated my opinion in the Muslim Ladies' magazine that none of the *Ikhwan* members should swear allegiance to a government whose legislation is not Allah's Law. I clearly stated that those members of the *Ikhwan* who accepted such posts should be expelled from the group. The *Ikhwan* had, in my opinion, to state clearly its position *vis-a-vis* the government's intentions.

Following a personal visit, 'Abd al-Qadir 'Awdah asked me to postpone any further writing about this issue. Indeed, I did refrain from such writings for a short period (two issues of our magazine appeared without discussing this problem). Yet, as I saw it, the issue was crucial and once again I began addressing it. 'Abd al-Qadir 'Awdah again visited me, but this time with an order from al-Hudaibi, asking me to stop my commentary. I recalled my pledge of allegiance to Hasan al-Banna - may Allah have mercy on his soul - and felt my loyalty incumbent in respect of his successor. I obeyed the order.

From then on, all my activities had to conform to my pledge of allegiance to the *Ikhwan*, even to the extent of requiring the *Murshid*'s prior consent for everything, including my participation in the Vienna Peace Conference.

The Veil Drops

Days went by, and the events of 1954 with all their calamities and ignominies. With them the mask concealing Nasir's face dropped away. His enmity towards Islam, through the war that he waged against Islamic activists and their leaders, was now very apparent. Death sentences were pronounced on giants of the Muslim *Ummah*: on *Shahid* 'Abd al-Qadir 'Awdah, the eminent Azharite and pious scholar, for whom the British authorities, back in 1951, offered a reward of E£10,000 to whomever delivered him dead or alive; on Shaykh Muhammad Farghali who was handed over dead to the British colonialists who had previously put a reward on his head but now had to volunteer nothing from their treasury. Countless other death sentences were issued and we should not forget any of these martyrs in the cause of Islam.

Even the great *Mujahid Imam* Hasan al-Hudaibi was sentenced to death. The sentence, however, was not carried out, for al-Hudaibi suffered a severe heart attack and was taken to hospital instead. With his condition critical the doctors declared he had only a few hours to live. Hearing this, Nasir issued a pardon for the *Murshid*, expecting to read his obituary in the papers the following morning. However, Allah's will dictated otherwise. Al-Hudaibi survived to provide the Muslims with an invaluable service, and to lead Islamic *da'wah*, albeit through its darkest period. He showed, despite suffering from many diseases and the tortures inflicted upon him, a strong and resolute firmness in following the truth. Despite being taken to a military prison where he was subjected to the most dreadful and inhuman atrocities, al-Hudaibi remained firm in adhering to truth, following the path of people who had carried great missions before him. He lived long enough to see the end of Nasir and his agents while standing firm and adhering only to *'azimah*. Not once did weakness creep into his heart, nor did he languor in the way of Allah. He refused to take *rukhsah* which would have allowed him to remain quiet in his house while his heart denounced what was happening elsewhere, as some scholars did by issuing *fatwas*.

I remember well his laudable and courageous stance when those who could no longer bear what was happening to them sought to adopt *rukhsah* by writing to the despot to demonstrate their support of him and to ask his pardon.

They asked al-Hudaibi to allow them to do this and his response can be recalled by many:

I do not force anyone to opt for *'azimah* and stand with us, but I say to you: missions have never been founded on those who opt for *rukhsah*.

Al-Hudaibi issued this famous statement at the ripe old age of 80, and whilst in prison at Turah Farm. He was one of the last of the *Ikhwan*'s members to be released, after Nasir's death.

Screams Calling Me to Duty!

I found myself, in 1955, recruited to serve Islamic *da'wah* without anyone's invitation. The screams of orphans who had lost their fathers under torture, the tears of widows who had lost their husbands behind prison bars, as well as the fathers and mothers whose children were killed by Nasir, haunted me. I felt as if I were responsible for the lost, the hungry, the dispossessed and the oppressed, and their numbers were increasing daily. The burden became too large for me to carry alone. For schools and universities required certain expenditure, landlords demanded their rents, and the problem was getting worse. The situation became even more acute when, in the middle of 1956, a number of brothers were acquitted and released from prison. Some of them were in dire need of money, food, clothing and shelter.

In desperation, I went to see my eminent teacher Shaykh Muhammad al-Awdan, one of the very few pure and pious people of al-Azhar. I was in the habit of consulting him in all *da'wah* affairs and issues related to Islamic learning. Like myself he held the view that the non-annexation of the Muslim Ladies Group might well serve the *Ikhwan* in the near future. The Shaykh was also aware

31

of my pledge to al-Banna which he both blessed and supported. He was also aware of my allegiance to *da'wah*.

I informed him about the tragedy surrounding the families of the *Ikhwan*'s members who had either been imprisoned or killed. I explained to him those things which I felt able to do for these people within the limits of my abilities. In short, as President of the Muslim Ladies Group, I would ensure as much help as possible for the *Ikhwan*'s families.

Shaykh Muhammad al-Awdan kissed my hand, saying: 'Don't hesitate to give any help you can. Allah is the One Who blesses endeavours.'

I reiterated to him my position *vis-à-vis* the group and the absolute trust that the Muslim Ladies had in me. His eminence confirmed my duty: 'It is now a conclusive obligation on you not to spare any effort in this respect, and to make what you are doing a secret between you and Allah. The only saviours of Islam - God willing - are those unfortunate *Ikhwan* members. We have no hope except in Allah and then in the sincerity of this group. Zainab, do whatever you can.'

And indeed, I did all that I could. I did not spare any effort, and yet no one was aware of it, for I would hand over all that I wanted to give to one or two persons only to distribute, and even then, I would make out that I was giving only what other people asked me to do on their behalf.

I found out later that the respected *Mujahidah*, wife of Hasan al-Hudaibi, was similarly expending a great deal of effort on behalf of these families as were other respected ladies from the *Ikhwan*'s sisters' branch such as the *Mujahidah* Amal al-'Ashmawi, wife of Munir al-Dallah and the '*Amirah* (head) of the Muslim Sisters, as well as Khalidah Hasan al-Hudaibi, Aminah Qutb, Hamidah Qutb, Fathiyyah Bakr, the *Mujahidah* Aminah al-Jawhari, 'Aliyah al-Hudaibi and Tahiyyah Sulaiman al-Hudaibi. Slowly, my contacts started to expand; in extreme secrecy I contacted Khalidah al-Hudaibi, then Hamidah and Aminah Qutb. All this for the sake of oppressed children and orphans.

'Abd al-Fattah Isma'il

My first encounter with 'Abd al-Fattah Isma'il took place in 1957, during the *Hajj* season. I was in al-Suwis port, with my brother Muhammad al-Ghazali al-Jubaili, on my way to Saudi Arabia in my capacity as head of the Muslim Ladies' delegation to *Hajj*, when I noticed him coming towards us. He was with another person, and his face radiated light and reverence. My brother introduced us, saying: 'This is 'Abd al-Fattah Isma'il, one of the dearest young Muslim brothers to Hasan al-Banna. He asked me to introduce him to you in this manner so that you would know him.'

'Abd al-Fattah Isma'il greeted me and told me that he would be with us on the same ship, then he left.

We boarded the ship and it was only a short time before we left the shore far behind. I busied myself with our delegation's needs only going to my room to rest after lunch. Then came a knock on my door and repeated requests to enter. Only when I had given my permission for the third time did my visitor enter. It was 'Abd al-Fattah Isma'il who, after greeting me, explained that he knew about my pledge to Hasan al-Banna after our long disagreement. I asked about the source of his information and he told me it was al-Banna himself. After further enquiries about what he wanted, he explained that he hoped I would meet him in Makkah, for the sake of Allah, to talk about what al-Banna wanted from me, God willing.

Although his expressions were smooth and easy they were imposing and did not leave room for one to think. Nevertheless, I informed him we could meet - God willing -

at the Muslim Ladies' place of stay in Makkah or Jeddah. He asked for these addresses so I referred him to Shaykh al-'Ashmawi and Mustafa al-'Alim, whom he said he knew, to give him my addresses in Makkah and Jeddah. He then greeted me and left.

One evening during the month of Dhul al-Hijjah, after 'Isha prayer, I had a meeting with his Eminence the late Shaykh Muhammad Bin Ibrahim, the then Grand *Mufti* of Saudi Arabia. I was reviewing with him a memorandum that I had presented to his Highness, the King, concerning the necessity of educating girls in the Saudi Kingdom, and asking him to hasten the implementation of this project, emphasizing its benefits for his country. The King had referred this memorandum to the Grand *Mufti*. Although the discussion lasted for two hours, I then headed towards Bab al-Salam with the intention of making *tawaf* of the *Ka'bah*. Suddenly someone called me with the greeting of Islam. It was 'Abd al-Fattah Isma'il and after asking me where I was heading, he accompanied me to the Mosque. After finishing the *tawaf* and praying two *rak'at*, we sat, facing *al-Multazim* (the door of the *Ka'bah*), to talk. He asked me: 'What do you think of the dissolution of the *Ikhwan*?'

'It is Islamically illegal.'

'This is exactly what I want to talk to you about.'

I asked Brother 'Abd al-Fattah Isma'il to come and see me at our place of stay, but he ruled this out as a convenient venue for such matters, for fear of Nasir's spies. We agreed to meet in the office of al-Haram al-Makki's building and, precisely, in the office of the righteous man Shaykh Salah al-Qazzaz. We did indeed meet there, but 'Abd al-Fattah secretly informed me that he preferred us to meet elsewhere, suggesting behind *maqam* Ibrahim.

After praying the *sunnah* of *tawaf*, we sat behind the Zamzam building, near *maqam* Ibrahim. He began speaking about the illegality of the *Ikhwan*'s dissolution

34

and the necessity of reorganizing the group and re-starting its activities. We agreed to continue our discussions immediately after we returned from *hajj*, and to seek Hasan al-Hudaibi, the *Murshid's* permission for this. As we were about to leave, he enjoined: 'We have to link ourselves here with a pledge of allegiance that we will fight in His sake and won't languor until we unite the ranks of the *Ikhwan*, and isolate all those who do not want to work for Him, no matter what their position or weight.'

We swore our allegiance to fight and die for the sake of His *Da'wah*, and shortly afterwards I returned to Egypt.

Permission to Work

By early 1958, my meetings with 'Abd al-Fattah Isma'il, both in my home and at the Muslim Ladies Headquarters, had become frequent. We would discuss Muslim affairs, trying with all our strength to do something that would bring back to the Muslim *Ummah* its *'aqidah* and past glory. As a point of reference we would use the *sirah* of the Prophet (peace be upon him) and the righteous *salaf* who came after him, making our way the way of the Qur'an and the *Sunnah*.

Our work plan included the gathering together of all those who wanted to work for Islam. Up until then we had confined ourselves to various research. From such efforts we had been able to conclude that Nasir's dissolution of the *Ikhwan* was void. Muslims were not bound by any pledge of allegiance to Nasir and should not, in any case, obey him for he was against Islam and did not take Allah's revelation for the country's legislation.

Now we required Hasan al-Hudaibi's permission to start our new works and after several meetings with him we were allowed to do so. The first step in our plan entailed 'Abd al-Fattah Isma'il making an exploratory trip throughout the whole of Egypt (districts, towns and villages) to identify those Muslims who would be fit to work with us. He was to begin with members of the *Ikhwan* so as to make them the nucleus of this grouping.

He began by contacting those Muslim brothers who came out of prison, so as to test their true colours, and to establish whether or not the trials the group had gone through had affected their will-power. We needed to know whether these formerly imprisoned Muslim brothers would try to avoid activities which might see them back in prison, whether their allegiance was still to the group and whether they remained ready to sacrifice everything dear to them for the sake of Allah and the defence of His religion.

This exploratory process was necessary to ensure our work began on firm ground with people really suited for it. Together we studied the reports that 'Abd al-Fattah presented about each region. I would then visit the *Murshid* to inform him about our findings and what we had agreed upon. If we mentioned any difficulties we were facing, his response would be: 'Carry on your march and do not look backwards. Don't be deceived by people's titles nor by their fame, for you are in the process of building a new structure from the bottom up.'

At times he would endorse what we presented to him, at others he would give us directives. Amongst these directives was the inclusion of *al-Muhalla* of Ibn Hazm in our list of study references.

By 1959, our researches culminated in the completion of our Islamic educational programmes. Dear reader, it is only right that I witness here, before Allah, that there was nothing in those programmes except matters dealing with the education of the Muslim individual. For the Muslim should know his duty towards his Lord and towards the formation of an Islamic society which is quite distinct from a non-Islamic society.

A Righteous Husband

My work on this project did not obstruct the fulfilment of my role at the Muslim Ladies Group, nor did it make me neglect my familial duties. However, when my respected husband, the late Muhammad Salim Salim, noticed Brother 'Abd al-Fattah Isma'il, together with a number of other pure Muslim youth, frequently visiting me at our home, he questioned: 'Is there *Ikhwan* activity here?'

'Yes.'

He asked me about the nature of this activity and its scope, and I answered that it was the re-organizing of the *Ikhwan* group. But when he began scrutinizing the matter further it was only correct that I reminded him of our undertakings to each other: 'Do you remember, my dear husband, what I told you when we agreed to marry?'

'Yes! You made some conditions, but I fear for you today because of your opposition to despots.'

'I remember very well what I told you. As we were going to be married I told you there was something in my life that you needed to know about so that you wouldn't ask me about it later on, for I will never relinquish it. I am the President of the Muslim Ladies Group, but some people think that I am a follower of al-Wafd political principles, which is not true. What I really believe in is the message of the *Ikhwan*. What relates me to Mustafa al-Nahhas is personal friendship, but I am under pledge of allegiance, until death for the sake of Allah, to Hasan al-Banna. Nevertheless, I have not stepped even one single step which would bestow upon me this divine honour. However, I believe one day I will take this step that I wish and dream of. If that day comes, and because of it, a clash is apparent between your personal interests and economic activities on the one hand, and my Islamic work on the other, and that I find my married

37

life is standing in the way of *da'wah* and the establishment of an Islamic state, then, each of us should go our own way.

'I expressed this to you then, and I remember well your tear-stained eyes and your questioning response: "I am asking you about your material requirements, you want none in respect of your dowry or marriage rights, but you ask me not to stop you from the way of Allah. I know of no link between you and Hasan al-Banna. In fact, I know that you disagreed with him concerning the annexation of the Muslim Ladies to the *Ikhwan* group."

'*Al-hamdu lillah*, I reached an agreement with Hasan al-Banna during the trial of 1948, shortly before he was martyred. I had decided, then, to relinquish the idea of getting married for ever, so that I would devote my entire life to *da'wah*. I cannot ask you today to share with me this struggle, but it is my right on you not to stop me from *jihad* in the way of Allah. Moreover, you should not ask me about my activities with other *mujahidin*, and let trust be full between us. A full trust between a man and a woman, a woman who, at the age of 18, gave her whole life to Allah and *da'wah*. In the event of any clash between the marriage contract's interest and that of *da'wah*, our marriage will end, but *da'wah* will always remain rooted in me.

'Do you remember all this, dear husband?'

'Yes.'

'I ask you today to keep your promise; do not ask me whom I meet and may Allah divide His reward for my efforts, if He accepts them, between us. I accept that ordering me to listen to you is amongst your rights, but Allah is greater than ourselves and His *da'wah* is dearer to us than ourselves. Besides, we are living in a dangerous phase of *da'wah*.'

'Forgive me. Carry on your work with Allah's blessing. If only I could live to see the establishment of an Islamic state and the *Ikhwan*'s goal achieved. If only I was still in my youth to work with you!'

Thereafter our work and activities intensified and a great many youth began visiting my house at all times of the day and night. My righteous husband would hear a knock on our door in the middle of the night. He would get up to answer it and let whoever was our visitor into the study-room. Then he would wake the woman, who was in charge of running our home affairs, to prepare tea and food for our visitors. Next he would wake me up with extreme care, saying: 'Some of your children are in the study-room, they look tired from travelling.'

Pulling on my clothes I would go and meet my visitors while my husband would go back to sleep, saying: 'Please wake me up, in case you pray *Fajr* in congregation, if it's all right with you.'

And, indeed, I would wake him up when we prayed in congregation. My husband always greeted all my visitors in a fatherly manner, full of love, care and compassion.

Contact with Shahid Sayyid Qutb

In 1962, I and 'Abd al-Fattah Isma'il, with al-Hudaibi's permission, met with the sisters of the great *mujahid*, *imam* and scholar Sayyid Qutb. We had approached his sisters so as to enlist their support for a meeting with the *Imam* to seek his instructions and advice concerning our research. To this end, I gave Hamidah Qutb a list of all the references that we were studying which included, among others, the *tafsir* of Ibn Kathir, *Al-Muhalla* of Ibn Hazm, *Al-Umm* of al-Shafi'i, books about *tawhid* and the *Fi zilal al-Qur'an* of Sayyid Qutb. After a while, Hamidah returned to us with a request that we study the introduction to the *tafsir* of *Surah al-An'am*, in its second edition. Furthermore she handed to me a folio which, she explained, was part of a book written by Sayyid whilst in prison and which was going to be published under the title *Ma'alim fi al-Tariq* (Milestones). When we had finished reading what she brought us, she would bring more.

I found out later that the *Murshid* had read Sayyid's manuscript and had given his permission for it to be published. When I asked the *Murshid* about it, he responded: 'With Allah's benediction, this book has confirmed all my trust in Sayyid, may Allah preserve him. Sayyid, Allah willing, is now the awaited hope for *da'wah.*'

We began our researches and studies anew in the form of small epistles which were distributed among the youth. These were then read and discussed in study circles. Ten to fifteen youth would gather to read ten verses of the Qur'an, then revise their injunctions and commands of behaviour as well as their goals and intentions for a Muslim life. When they had understood and grasped these verses another ten would be studied and so on, following the example of the Companions of the Prophet (peace be upon him).

Sweet, glorious days and Allah's bounties passed by while we studied and taught ourselves, as well as preparing our youth for *da'wah*. It was of paramount importance that we prepare future generations in the persons of these youth who would hopefully become teachers of education and training in their own right for subsequent generations.

We had decided, following Sayyid Qutb's instructions and with the consent of al-Hudaibi, to extend the period of education, training and planting of *tawhid* in people's hearts, to thirteen years. This accorded with *da'wah*'s age in Makkah. The grassroots of the Muslim *Ummah* in Egypt were members of the *Ikhwan* who adhered to the *Shari'ah* of Allah. We were bound to establish all the commands mentioned in the Qur'an and the *Sunnah* inside our Islamic circle. Obedience was due to our sworn-in *imam*, with however, a postponement of implementing the *hudud*[8] until the establishment of an Islamic state, despite our belief in these *hudud* and our defence of them. We were also convinced that the earth was, then, devoid of any base that had the characteristic of an entirely devoted Islamic *Ummah*, as was the case with the period of the righteous caliphate. *Jihad* was obligatory as it was on any Muslim community which wants the establishment of Allah's rule and its firm implementation, until all Muslims come back to Islam, and the religion of God is upheld, not as slogans but as a practical, living reality.

We studied the state of all the Muslim world, looking for examples that compared with the righteous caliphate whose model we wanted to implement. We decided, after a long study of the bitter realities, however, that there was not a single Islamic state that deserved to be that example, with the exception of Saudi Arabia. Even then we had some reservations, feeling this country needed to undertake some emendations and corrections before it could be truly exemplary. All our studies showed that the nation of Islam was not upheld, even though various states waved slogans claiming it had established the *Shari'ah* of Allah.

It was decided after these exhaustive studies, that after thirteen years of Islamic training of our youth, elders, women and children, we would make an exhaustive survey of the state. If this survey revealed that at least 75% of the followers of *da'wah* believed that Islam is a complete way of life and are convinced about establishing an Islamic state, then we would call for the establishment of such a state. If the percentage is less, then we would extend the period of Islamic training for another thirteen years and so on, until the *Ummah* is ripe to accept Islam's rule.

We were not at all bothered about the time this would take. What was important was that we carried on working until our deaths and that the banner of 'there is no God but Allah and Muhammad is His Messenger' is handed over to those who would come after us.

We were also, with the permission of Hasan al-Hudaibi, in contact with Muhammad Qutb. He would visit me at my home, at Misr al-Jadidah, to explain to the youth issues that were obscure to them. Indeed, the youth asked him many questions which he gladly answered.

Notes

1. The first Arab-Israeli war. The *Ikhwan* committed a great many of their men and youth to this war.

2. My master. A title of respect which can also mean Sir, or my lord.

3. A social, athletic and cultural Islamic organization formed in 1927.

4. Mustafa al-Nahhas (1876-1965) was the leader of the Nationalist Wafd party, and as such was a dominant figure in Egyptian politics until the 1952 revolution. He was five times Egypt's Prime Minister.

5. Egyptian statesman and King Faruq's uncle.

6. Army officer and statesman, and first Egyptian President after the 1952 *coup*. He played a prominent role in the revolutionary overthrow of King Faruq I, before being arrested by Nasir and put under house confinement.

7. He was deputy leader of the *Ikhwan*, but left the group to become Nasir's Minister for Endowment and Religious Affairs.

8. *Hudud* (sing. *hadd*) (lit. limit, borderline, ordinance). A legal term for the offences and punishments which are defined in the Qur'an.

CHAPTER 3

Conspiracy

Six months after the failed attempt to kill me, Sayyid
Qutb was released. Quickly thereafter, news began
circulating to the effect that Sayyid Qutb's release had
been planned by the Secret Services so as to facilitate his
assassination; we had come to learn of a plan to liquidate
some leading Islamic figures, among them 'Abd al-Fattah
Isma'il. We continued our work, placing our reliance on
Allah, while the despots sought all means to prevent us.
We were aware, through information that had come our
way, that the governing bodies had assumed that there
was an Islamic intellectual movement being led from
within prison by Sayyid Qutb. Furthermore, they believed
a secret organization in the *Ikhwan* was controlled outside
by 'Abd al-Fattah Isma'il and myself.
We were aware that both the American and Soviet
Secret Service agencies, along with their international
Zionist ally, had presented reports to Nasir with
recommendations to address the problems presented by
the Islamic Movement with the utmost urgency. Should
Nasir fail, the reports concluded, then his achievement in
renouncing Islamic thought and in nullifying any thoughts
people may have had about the possibility of reformation
through Islam in the region, would all be swept away.
For Nasir, an Islamic renaissance would be a terrible

43

blow to his tyrannical, dictatorial style of leadership.

I received news, in early August 1965, of a list of all those who were to be arrested from the new Islamic education programme's squadron. Remember, dear reader, this squadron was comprised of youth who were beams of light moving with Islam in the same manner as the first generation of Muslims in Dar al-Arqam, and were under the leadership of Sayyid Qutb, 'Abd al-Fattah Isma'il, Muhammad Yusuf Hawash and myself.

On 5th August, Sayyid Qutb was again arrested. A few days earlier Muhammad Qutb had been incarcerated in Marsa Matruh prison. Pending developments and fearing subsequent arrests, further meetings of the Muslim Ladies Group were postponed. In any case, following Sayyid Qutb's arrest the question of who would succeed to his responsibilities was one only the *Murshid* could answer.

'Abd al-Fattah Isma'il and I had considered such eventualities only five days before they happened. When they did, he came to visit me asking that I travel to Alexandria to discuss the situation with the *Murshid*. He also introduced me to one of our youth, who would act as our liaison-point should 'Abd al-Fattah himself be arrested. Only hours later, I received a message from him asking me to cancel my trip and stay at home. It was too late, for I had already contacted the *Murshid*. Before long the *Murshid*'s wife came to see me. It was agreed that I should maintain continuous contact with the *Murshid* and to facilitate this I was introduced to a brother by the name of Mursi Mustafa Mursi.

During the next few days thousands of Muslims were arrested. Some later reports attested that one hundred thousand members of the *Ikhwan* were arrested in just a 20-day span. Al-Qal'ah, the military prison, as well as Za'bal Prison, al-Fayyum and Tanta prisons and others were filled with our Muslim brothers. And on Thursday 19th August, a respected 85-year-old lady, Umm Ahmad, was also arrested. A woman who had accompanied *da'wah* from the very first day, and who had walked, step by step, in the way of Hasan al-Banna, she had performed many good works in helping those families who had lost their breadwinners to Nasir's prisons. In an attempt to comfort her nephew and attest to Umm Ahmad's sincerity, I reminded him of her strength: 'It is a beautiful thing, that there is on this earth a believing woman, in her 86th year, who has been arrested for the sake of Allah and the state of the Qur'an. Bravo! Bravo!, O soldiers of Allah!'

Immediately after, I sent for my daughter in Islam, Ghadah 'Amar: 'Today, an eminent, respected *Mujahidah*, Umm Ahmad, who lives in Shabra, has been arrested. In case I should be arrested, I want you to hand over the money in this envelope to either the *Murshid* or Qutb's family. It belongs to the families of those who are imprisoned and is for *da'wah*.'

I handed the package containing the group's money to her. It had been collected via the *Ikhwan*'s members' regular membership fee, and had been deposited with me in trust. Subsequently, and after my arrest, I learned that Ghadah had handed over this money to my daughter in Islam, Fatimah 'Isa, and that it had been taken by the despot's agents when she, too, was arrested. This money had been destined to help pay for food, and pay the rents, health and education expenses of the families of those imprisoned and their children.

My Turn!

At dawn on Friday 20th August, the despot's men invaded my house. Asking to see a search warrant, I was met with the following rebuff: 'Warrant! What warrant you fool? We live in the time of Nasir. We can do whatever we like to you, you dog!'

Then they began laughing hysterically, and by further insult added: 'The *Ikhwan* are crazy. They expect a search warrant in Nasir's rule!'

Then they began tearing up and breaking everything in the house, leaving nothing intact. I watched silently, monitoring their contempt. Next, they arrested my nephew, Muhammad Muhammad al-Ghazali, a student at the Teachers' College (Kulliah al-Mu'allimin), who was staying with me as a son. When they had finished, they turned to me, saying: 'Do not leave your house, you B...... .'

'Do I understand from this that I am under house confinement?'

'Yes. Until further orders! And know that we are watching you and your house. If you move from it we will arrest you.'

I thought that was the end of the matter. But by way of precaution, and just as my sister, her husband and children came to visit me, I began preparing a suitcase to take with me should I be arrested. I begged my brother-in-law and family to leave, fearing that they too would be arrested if the despot's agents returned. They insisted on staying.

Soon my worst fears were confirmed. Nasir's agents returned, this time taking everything from the family safe. Informed that the keys to the safe were with my husband and he was away on holiday, like thieves in the night, they had brought their own cutting equipment to secure entry. When I asked for a receipt for the safe's contents, as much belonged to my husband, I was again mockingly reminded that Nasir's agents did not give receipts. Being smart, I was told, would get me nowhere so I should just shut my mouth. Next they took more than half my personal library, despite my attempts to save some old volumes of *Tafsir*, *Fiqh* and *Hadith* that had been published more than a century earlier. Nor did my attempts succeed to keep three sets of the Muslim Ladies' magazine which, as you will recall, had been suspended by a military order in 1958. Everything and anything they wanted was confiscated.

I was not at all surprised, therefore, that my arrest followed. I was shoved inside a lorry where I found my nephew and another youth of *da'wah*.

'How is everything, Muhammad?', I asked.

He did not answer me, so I realized that he had been ordered not to speak. They had brought my nephew along only to show them the way to my home, for these agents were other than my previous dawn visitors.

I recognized the Military prison from the sign on its outside gate. We passed through and I was taken from the lorry and pushed into a room where another scoundrel began questioning me. I stood in front of a huge man with a gloomy countenance and an impertinent way of talking. He asked the person forcibly holding me by my arm who I was, but even then he turned towards me, asking harshly: 'Who are you?'

'Zainab al-Ghazali.'

He began swearing and cursing in the most filthy and unthinkable way. The person holding my arm screamed at me: 'This is the Chief Prosecutor you B.......!, answer him.'

The Chief Prosecutor remained silent while I answered: 'You have arrested me, confiscated my books and everything that was in our safe. I request you to bring all these things here and record them so that they can be returned later to me.'

The Chief Prosecutor, whom I knew later as Shams Badran, answered perversely and with an arrogant lowliness: 'You B......! We are going to kill you in an hour. What books, safe and receipt are you talking about? We're going to hang you in a little while! We're going to bury you B.....! in the same way we buried, here in the

Military prison, tens of scores of your likes, you dogs!'

Unable to answer his violent and filthy verbiage, I looked on as he raised his voice and ordered my restrainer to take me away.

'Where to?'

'They know!'

The pervert grabbed me savagely by the arm, saying: 'You B.......!'

Inwardly, I prayed: 'I seek refuge in Allah from the accursed Satan. O Allah! Bestow on me Your tranquillity, and hold firm my steps within the circles of the people of truth, and give me strength by means of Your remembrance, and provide me with contentment for that which pleases You.'

The wretched man continued to hold my arm and took me to another room where two men sat at a desk. One of the men held an agenda which I immediately recognized as belonging to Brother *Shahid* 'Abd al-Fattah Isma'il. He had used it during our Qur'anic studies for writing down his remarks. Thus, I knew that 'Abd al-Fattah Isma'il, as well as the other brothers with whom he had a meeting had also been arrested. I felt myself begin to tremble and feared that my oppressors would notice this.

The call for *'Asr* prayer from the Mosque outside the prison walls reached my ears. I silently prayed, not wishing it to be noticed. Thankfully, I finished before being taken to Room 24.

The Way to Room 24

On my way to Room 24, accompanied by two men holding whips, I was deliberately taken past different places inside the prison such that I could see for myself the hideous things taking place there. Almost unable to believe my eyes and not wanting to accept such inhumanity, I silently watched as members of the *Ikhwan* were suspended in the air and their naked bodies ferociously flogged. Some were left to the mercy of savage dogs which tore at their bodies. Others, with their face to the wall awaited their turn. Worse still, I knew many of these pious, believing youth personally. They were as dear to me as my own sons, and had attended study circles of *Tafsir* and *Hadith* in my home, in their own homes and at Ibn al-Arqam house.

One by one, these youth of Islam, shaikhs of Islam, were tortured, left standing with their face to the wall, and flogged ferociously. Some had blood running down their foreheads. Foreheads that did not bow to anyone except Allah. The light of *Tawhid* shone from their raised faces, proud to belong to the cause of Allah.

One of them shouted to me: 'Mother! May Allah make you firm!'

'Sons! It is a pledge of allegiance. Be patient Yasir's family, your reward is Paradise.'[1]

The man with me struck me so hard on my head that I felt my eyes and ear turning as if hit by an electrical force. And the light from inside the prison made me aware of the many, many more tortured bodies filling the place. - '[Let it be] for the sake of Allah!'

'Let it be for the sake of Allah!', I braved.

At that moment, a voice, as if coming from Paradise, could be heard saying: 'O Allah! Hold their steps firm and protect them from the perverts. Had it not been for You, O Lord!, we would not have been guided. Nor would we have prayed nor given anything in charity. So, please hold our steps firm in trial and in adversity.'

The sound of flogging became louder and more intense, but the voice of *iman* was both stronger and clearer. Another voice rallied: 'There is no god but Allah.'

And, I again repeated: 'Patience my sons, it is a pledge of allegiance. Patience, your reward is Paradise.'

I was struck sharply on my back but I would not

relent: 'Allah is the Greatest, praise be to Allah. O Allah! Give us patience and contentment. Praise and thanks are due to You, O Allah! For the bounties of Islam, *Iman* and *Jihad* in Your way which You bestowed upon us.'

The door to a dark room was opened, I was hurled inside, and the door crashed shut behind me.

Inside Room 24

'In the Name of Allah, peace be upon you!', I repeated.

The next moment the door was locked and a bright light switched on. Now their purpose was revealed; the room was full of dogs! I could not count how many!

Scared, I closed my eyes and put my hands to my chest. Within seconds the snarling dogs were all over me, and I could feel their teeth tearing into every part of my body. Clenching my hands tight into my armpits, I began to recount the Names of Allah, beginning with 'O Allah! O Allah!' The dogs were unrelenting, digging their teeth into my scalp, my shoulders, back, chest and wherever another had not already taken hold. I repeatedly invoked my Lord, calling: 'O Lord! Make me not distracted by anything except You. Let all my attention be for You Alone, You my Lord, the One, the Only, the Unique, the Eternal Absolute. Take me from the World of Forms. Distract me from all these phenomena. Let my whole attention be for You. Make me stand in Your Presence. Bestow on me Your Tranquillity. Clothe me with the garments of Your Love. Provide me with death for Your sake, loving for Your sake, contentment with You. O Lord! Hold the steps of the faithful firm.'

I repeated this inwardly for what seemed like several hours until at last the door was opened, the dogs forced from my body and I was taken out.

I expected that my clothes would be thoroughly stained with blood, for I was sure the dogs had bitten every part of my body. But, incredulously, there was not a single blood-stain on my clothes, as if the dogs had been in my imagination only. May God be exalted! He is with me. I began questioning inwardly whether I deserved all these bounties and gifts from Allah. My warders could not believe it either. I glimpsed the sky outside filled with evening twilight, indicating sunset. I concluded that I must have been locked in with the dogs for more than three hours. Praise be to God for any adversity!

I was pushed, and staggered along for what seemed a long time. A door was opened, and I felt lost in the vast hall which it gave onto. I was led along another long corridor, past many closed doors. I noticed one of these doors slightly ajar, and giving out enough light to brighten the obscurity of the corridor. Through it I caught a glimpse of the illuminated face of Muhammad Rashad Mahna, once Egypt's Crown Prince. The Nasir regime believed that the *Ikhwan* would install him as Head of State if they took over power. Hence his arrest. Cell No. 3, next to Cell No. 2, was opened and I was hurled inside.

Cell No. 3

The door was locked behind me, and immediately the lamp hanging from the cell's roof lit. The sheer intensity of the light was enough to terrify and intimidate. It could only mean further barbarism and torture.

After a while I knocked on the door and a gloomy-faced demon harshly wanted to know what for. I asked permission to go to the toilet to make my ablutions. Ignominy of ignominies, I was not allowed to knock on the door, nor was I allowed to go to the toilet, nor make ablutions, nor allowed to drink.

'Knock on the door again, you B......!, and I'll flog you 50 times.' He hit the air with his whip, to demonstrate his eager readiness to carry out his threat.

In my bare cell, exhausted from my ordeal in Room 24, I took off my coat, spreading it out on the floor. I did *tayammum*, prayed *Maghrib* and *'Isha* and sat still. My leg, still painful from the operation was beginning to trouble me, so, placing my shoes underneath my head, I lay down.

The silence was soon broken by the sounds of a wooden post being erected outside my cell window. Then, one believing youth after another was brought, strapped to the post in the crucifixion position and beaten ferociously. Each in turn would invoke Allah, asking for His help. After half an hour or so of this intensive whipping their torturers would ask each youth, many of them engineers, doctors or councillors, when they had arrived here.

'Today or yesterday', was the response.

'When did you last go to Zainab al-Ghazali's house?'

If these brothers said they could not remember, the butchers would continue their torture, demanding that they curse me with the most despicable, lowly expressions. Of course, the brothers would refuse, and the flogging continued unabated. Some, brave enough and strong enough to say that they had not observed in me anything except sincerity and good virtues, were beaten unconscious. All this to break my resolve and will. I began invoking Allah, begging Him for His mercy. I cried out for the butchers to torture me instead of these youth, for I thought it would be less painful for me. I began asking Allah to put me in their place, to spare me as well as these brothers from such heinous torture. I begged that my brethren should say what the butchers wanted to hear such that they could be spared further pain. But they did not, staying steadfast in their refusals. The floggings multiplied, the cries of anguish increased and my shame at what was being done was immeasurable.

From my compassion and grief, I continued to invoke Allah, saying: 'O Allah! Make it such that by my attentions to You I am distracted from them, and make it such that by their attention to You they are distracted from me. Lord! Inspire them to do good deeds You are pleased with. Lord! Shield from me the cries of these tortures. Lord! You know what is within me and I do not know what is within You and You are the most Knower of the unseen. You know people's innermost secrets and what breasts hide. Lord! Have mercy on Your people!'

The Vision

I do not know how but I fell asleep while invoking Allah, and it was then that I experienced the first of four visions of the Prophet (peace be upon him) that I was to see during my stay in prison. There in front of me, praise be to Allah, was a vast desert and camels with hawdahs as if made of light. On each hawdah were four men, all with luminous faces. I found myself behind this huge train of camels in that vast, endless desert, and standing behind a great, reverent man. This man was holding a halter which passed through the neck of each camel. I wondered silently: Could this man be the Prophet (peace be upon him)?

Silence has no safeguard with the Prophet, who replied: 'Zainab! You are following in the footsteps of Muhammad, Allah's Servant and Messenger.'

'Am I, master! Following in the footsteps of Muhammad, Allah's Servant and Messenger?'

'You, Zainab Ghazali, are following in the footsteps of Muhammad, Allah's Servant and Messenger.'

'O my Beloved! Am I truly following in your footsteps?'

'Zainab! You are on the right path. You are on the right path, Zainab! You are following in the footsteps of Muhammad, Allah's Servant and Messenger.'

Twice more I repeated my question, receiving the same response from the Prophet.

I woke up feeling I owned the world. Astonished, I had

forgotten my whereabouts and what I was facing. Nor did I feel any pain nor see the wooden post near the window. It seemed that I had been taken to another place whereof voices came from a far. Furthermore, I was also astonished for, although I am known as Zainab al-Ghazali, my recorded name at birth was Zainab Ghazali, and it was by this name that the Prophet had called me. Indeed, the vision had transported me beyond time and space. I did *tayammum* and began praying, thanking Allah for this gift. In one of my prostrations I found myself invoking: 'Lord! By what means am I going to thank You? There is nothing I can thank You with except by renewing my allegiance to You. O Allah! I pledge allegiance to die for Your Sake. O Allah! I pledge allegiance to You that none should be tortured because of me. O Allah! Hold me firm in following the truth that You are pleased with, and confine me within the limits of right that pleases You!'

Tranquillity and peace of mind were mine.

I heard a commotion outside. The noise of countless lorries arriving filled with a new shift of butchers whilst others left, their duties for the time being completed. A new wave of torture would soon begin. I could hear the *Adhan* of *Fajr*, and so made *tayammum* and prayed.

I remained in my cell for six consecutive days: from Friday 20th August to Thursday 26th August, 1965. My cell door, during these six days was never opened. I was given neither food, drink, allowed to go to the toilet nor any contact with the outside world, except my warder who, now and then, peeped through the small hole in my cell door. You can imagine, dear reader, how a person can live in such circumstances. For if one can do without food and drink, one cannot do without going to the toilet. Remember also, that all this took place during August! Would Judaism or even Paganism allow such treatment, let alone by people claiming to be Muslims? Could such things be possible?

O Allah! How often did these despotic dictators abuse human dignity and wash their hands of any and all religion and morals. For the oppressed, however, certainty in Allah, belief in truth and living guided by one's Lord produce strength capable of transcending such degradation. Therefore dear reader, don't be amazed that I could live for six days without water, food, or going to the toilet. Indeed I was able to survive for those six days because of two things:

Firstly, it is Allah's favour on us that we believe in Him. Islam bestows us with a strength which helps us to surmount problems and difficulties. This is Allah's favour. *Iman* gives tremendous strength and energy for bearing hardships. A strength beyond that of those perverse despots who think it is they who truly rule. The believer lives in contact with Allah, independently of shape or form.

Secondly, it was that blessed vision which was like food or a tonic from Allah which enabled me to live in distraction from all that was happening around me. It was this which helped me endure, in submission and acceptance, this earthly hell.

On the morning of the seventh day, my guard brought some water, a quarter of bread stained with human excrement and a piece of yellow cheese. He threw these onto the floor, shouting: 'B......! Since you are still alive, this is your food!'

I touched neither the bread nor the cheese, but I took of the water despite the filthy pot in which it was brought, blocking my nose to reduce the stench from the pot and saying: 'In the Name of Allah with Whose name nothing can harm neither on earth nor in heaven, and He is the All-Hearing, All-Knowing. O Allah! Let it be food, water, effort, learning, patience and submission.'

I slowly drank the water. Then, just before sunset my

warder entered my cell, hitting the walls and floor with his whip.

'Get up B......! You can go to the toilet!', he yelled.

I tried to get up but fell back from sheer exhaustion. The warder pulled me up roughly by the arm and walked me there himself but, as I tried to close the toilet door, he shouted: 'You're not allowed to close it!'

'Take me back to my cell then, I don't want anything.'

'Get in B......! How should we watch over you!', he retorted savagely, his insolence matched only by his pleasure at my humiliation.

What immorality or what *Jahiliyyah*[2] could allow this kind of behaviour?

I went back to my cell wishing only to die, for death would be better than dancing to my captors' evil tune again. As the cell door closed behind me, I quickly made *tayammum* and prayed *Maghrib* and '*Isha*. No sooner had I finished, than the beast who had previously taken me to the dogs, his name Safwat al-Rubi, darkened my cell door, accompanied by two others.

'Please, come in doctor', I heard him say.

One of the two men examined me, while I lay on the cell floor.

'So, how is she Sha'rawi?', the third enquired.

'Nothing, her heart is well.'

Needing no further confirmation as to my health, they left the cell, and the door was locked. Later, I was to suffer a heart blood-clot because of the torture they inflicted upon me.

My respite was only temporary, for within minutes I was taken to a vast, dark room, similar to a court room, where I was left for nearly two hours facing the wall. I was ordered not to move, and I recall their words as they left me there: 'B........! You are going to die today!'

I took their threat seriously, praying to Allah for tranquillity and peace and to take me to Him as a Muslim.

I had memorized *al-Fatihah* and *al-Baqarah* and now began to recount these *surahs* in such a way that I was hearing them for the first time.

I was abruptly awakened from my recitation by a strong and painful slap. The lights were switched on and a brute of a man began flogging me with the utmost ferocity. Darkness oozed from this man's face, as if his eyes held the devil incarnate. He then gave me three blank pieces of paper and a pen, saying: 'Write on these papers.'

At that moment three other men entered the room demanding that I be flogged again: 'B.........! This is in order that you don't forget what we want you to write.' Then the flogging stopped and one of them - I knew him later as Hamzah al-Basyuni - took hold of me roughly, and threw me against the wall. Another shook me violently until I fell to the floor and it was he who ordered the soldier to kick me.

Forced to a chair, I was made to sit and again given blank pieces of paper. I could hardly hold them because of the pain that was tearing my limbs apart. One of my incarcerators shouted: 'Write the names of all the people you know in Saudi Arabia, Syria, Sudan, Lebanon, Jordan and in any other part of the world. Write down the names of all your acquaintances on the face of this earth. If you don't, we will shoot you where you stand. Write down the names of all your *Ikhwan* acquaintances and everything about your relationship with them.'

They then left the cell, closing the door behind them.

I wrote: 'I have many friends, in many countries, who have known me through Islamic *da'wah*. Our movements on this earth are for Allah, and He leads those who choose His path. This path is the same as that which the Prophet (peace be upon him) and his Companions followed before us. Our aim is to spread Allah's message and to call for the implementation of His rule. I call you, in the Name of Allah, to leave your *Jahiliyyah*, renew your Islam, pronounce the *shahadah* and submit and repent to Allah from this darkness that has swathed your hearts, and which prevents you from doing any good deed. If you do so, perhaps Allah will take you out of this abyss of *Jahiliyyah* and bring you to the light of Islam. Communicate this message to your President, such that he may repent, ask forgiveness, and come back to Islam, ridding himself of his *Jahiliyyah*. If he refuses, remember, you are still responsible for yourselves and the way you have chosen. I bear witness that there is no god but Allah and I bear witness that Muhammad is His Servant and Messenger. O Allah! May You be a witness that I have conveyed Your Message. If they repent, please accept their repentance and ours, but if they ignore it, You are the Exalted in might, the Wise. O Allah! Hold firm our steps in Your way and bestow on us, by Your gift and favour, martyrdom for Your Sake.'

I wrote with the help of Allah, trusting that I had performed His Message. Once I had finished, I recommenced my invocation of Him.

Eventually, Safwat al-Rubi returned and took away what I had written. The lights were switched off and I was again left alone in that frightening hole. However, only a few moments could have passed when four men came rushing into my cell, Safwat al-Rubi among them, shouting his usual, dirty verbiage: 'You B.......! B.........! B..........! Do you think we're joking? What's this nonsense you've written?' Then, 'Attention! Hamzah al-Basyuni, Director General of military prisons.'

Hamzah al-Basyuni entered accompanied by his own brand of debased swearing, words which were lower than anything I had heard so far in that prison. I looked at him with utter disgust and contempt. One of his sidekicks had a paper in his hand which he falsely claimed was the one I had written. Another man tore this up as Basyuni said: 'Take her, there's no hope for her.'

As Basyuni and his party left, more soldiers entered my cell. I was thrown savagely across the floor and, before I realized what was happening, they had tied my hands and feet and suspended me from a wooden post, the same way a butcher would hang a slaughtered sheep. I was flogged savagely. My torturers, trained for such crimes, lashed my body with their whips time and time again. I repeated the name of Allah until I became unconscious.

I regained consciousness to find myself on a stretcher, unable to move or speak but nevertheless aware of what was going on. I again passed out and, on coming to, realized that I had suffered a severe haemorrhage. I knocked on my cell door asking for help to stem the bleeding and for a doctor. I received only more curses and foul language.

I went back to my Lord, asking Him, He Who has everything in His Hands, to lift away from me what I was going through. I remembered the *Hadith* of the Prophet (peace be upon him): 'Avoid the supplication (prayers) of the oppressed [against you], for there is no veil between it and Allah.'[3] I asked Allah to stop the haemorrhage, and by His Magnanimity and Favour He granted my prayer. I continued to seek His refuge in prayer, and as a means of distracting my mind from the severity of the pain from my beaten body. I remained in that condition for many days. No doctor, no treatment, nothing but an occasional piece of bread or cheese thrown into my cell by that devil of a guard. Unable to stand their smell, even these few morsels remained untouched.

But Allah Has United Them

One day, I felt compelled towards the door of my cell, for I heard footsteps which my heart felt inclined to. I looked through the hole which the guard used for checking on me from time to time, and I saw *Imam*

Hasan al-Hudaibi, the *Murshid* al-'Am. He, too, had been arrested. Without hesitation, I put my lips to the hole in the door and mouthed: *'So lose not heart, nor fall into despair: for you must gain mastery if you are true in faith. If a wound has touched you, be sure a similar wound has touched the others . . .'*[4] Thereafter I anticipated the *Murshid's* dear footsteps every day, and Allah enabled me to see him. On each occasion I would mouth the same verse and he would answer by means of a slight inclination of his head which the guard accompanying him never noticed.

This daily event gave me tremendous heart, and enabled me to forget all my pains. This feeling could not, of course, be apprehended except by those who are brothers in Allah. For Islam forms a link between its leadership and soldiers, a link which transcends individual egos and makes the pleasure of Allah the goal of all. I lived in peace with that knowledge.

Back to the Vortex

The tranquillity was short-lived. One afternoon, Safwat al-Rubi entered my cell and began lashing out at everything, including the walls, with his whip. He took me savagely by the arms and dragged me to that dreadful hall, and from there to an office facing Cell No. 2. He made me sit in a chair facing a desk and promptly left. Soon came another man, asking me whether I was Zainab al-Ghazali and when I answered in the affirmative he left. Shortly after, three soldiers entered, each looking as though he had just come from Hell: they were unusually tall and muscular and their faces reflected the harshness of their hearts. Another man also entered, telling me as he did: 'The hour of your death has come!'

I closed my eyes and began silent preparations for my end, only to find that my tormentors had left. What agonies and cruelties they knew how to inflict! Their cruel methods were just beginning to register, when they returned with one of my brothers in Islam, Faruq al-Manshawi. They tied him up and hung him as if to be crucified, on a wooden post. Then the flogging began. Between each session they would ask him about the number of times he had visited me. Then, they would ask him to curse me. He would refuse and the flogging would continue. My heart cried at what I saw and heard.

The butchers continued their work until I thought al-Manshawi must be dead. But Allah decided that it was to be otherwise. For he lived, only to be later sentenced to life imprisonment. From his cell, he would call people to Islam and to the truth that he believed in. Unable to stand for any more, Nasir ordered his assassination in Liman Turah Prison.

As if their sins against Brother Faruq were not enough, they then brought another brother and asked him the same things as they had asked Faruq. This brother, too, refused. The torture intensified until eventually, thinking he was dying, they put him on a stretcher and took him away.

It seems my accusers thought I would be persuaded, because of what I saw and heard, into answering all their questions. They even sent along a man who pretended to have my best interests at heart. Introducing himself as 'Umar 'Isa, prosecuting attorney, he began his advice saying: 'Hajjah Zainab! I want to reach an agreement with you so as to save you from the grip of these trials. How can you throw yourself away in this disgusting manner while being who you are, Zainab al-Ghazali the respected, the protected lady? Look! All the Ikhwan's members, including al-Hudaibi, have confessed to everything. They have all said things about you which means your certain death. They've protected themselves by incriminating you. My opinion Hajjah, is that you should rectify your position before it's too late. Tell them the truth about what these people were about to do and clarify your position, for I'm sure that your position was always right.'

I remained silent.

'Answer me Madam Zainab. We want to know the truth.'

'Neither the *Ikhwan*, nor myself, have done anything which displeases Allah. In fact, we have not done anything that would displease normal people who grasp the truth. What have we done? We teach people about Islam. Is this a crime?'

'But their statements show they were conspiring to do many other things including assassinate Nasir and sabotage the country. Moreover, it was you who instigated them to do so. I am a prosecuting attorney, my only goal is to reach the truth. Now, what do you think?'

'It is not the *Ikhwan*'s goal to kill Nasir or anybody else. Nor is it their goal to sabotage the country. The one who has sabotaged the country is Nasir himself. Our goal is greater than that. Our goal is universal truth: the case of *Tawhid* on earth, the *Tawhid* of Allah, the worship of Allah alone, the establishment of the Qur'an and the *Sunnah*. There is no sovereignty except that of God. When our goal is achieved, God willing, the unbelievers' idols will be destroyed and their legend will end. Our goal is reformation not sabotage, edification not destruction.'

The man smiled slowly, saying:

'This means that you really are conspiring against Nasir and his rule. This is evident from what you have said *Hajjah* Zainab.'

'Islam does not know the language of conspiracy but confronts falsehood with the truth and makes a distinction for people between two ways: the way of Allah and the way of the devil. Those who follow the devil's way are miserable, sick people, so we give them their cure with care and affection. This cure is the call to Allah, the religion of Allah, the laws of Allah. (*We send down in the Qur'an that which is a healing and mercy to those who believe: to the unjust it causes nothing but loss after loss.*)'

The face of the man claiming to be the prosecuting attorney changed colour and as he left the room, still holding to his falsehood, he said: 'I only wanted to help you, but it seems you are still deceived by what the *Ikhwan* have convinced you of.'

I later learned, as I had in any case surmised, that this so-called prosecuting attorney was nothing more than another of Nasir's miserable tools; his name, Sa'd Abd al-Karim.

Safwat al-Rubi then returned and made me stand facing the wall for several hours. All I could hear were the continuous howls of pain and anguish as one after another of the *Ikhwan*'s members underwent the most barbarous torture. The names of Mursi Mustafa, Faruq al-Sawi and Tahir 'Abd al-'Aziz Salim are here recalled. The so-called prosecuting attorney returned, this time with Hamzah al-Basyuni and Safwat al-Rubi.

'Why don't you want to reach an agreement with the prosecuting attorney?', said Hamzah. 'We want to save you from the mess you're in. I know your husband. He's a good man and you're going to get him into deep trouble. Hasan al-Hudaibi and the brothers have said everything. Why don't you save yourself like they have?'

'True! The *Ikhwan*'s members have said everything. That's why you continue to flog and crucify them. I won't lie for the *Ikhwan*, nor for myself. We are Muslims working for Islam and this is our work.'

At this the butchers standing behind their lieutenants began hitting the floor with their whips. I said to the so-called prosecuting attorney: 'What about these whips, prosecuting attorney, are they from the law school curriculum?'

Hamzah al-Basyuni struck me hard on the face, saying:

'Eh! Do you want to make us crazy? I can bury you like I bury ten of the likes of you every day.'

I looked once more at the so-called prosecuting attorney: 'Why don't you write this in your minutes, that is if you have any?'

Hamzah al-Basyuni glared at me ferociously: 'That's it, you can deal with her yourselves. I wanted to help her but she refuses.'

His words were like orders to Safwat and his butchers. They flogged me continuously, their whips striking savagely one after the other across my body while I raised my voice to Allah: 'O Allah! Help me! Bestow peace on me!'

A few hours later Safwat came back with a man called 'Sambo', who hit me on the face repeatedly, and then dragged me to my cell.

Then, at the *Adhan* of *Fajr*, I prayed, raising my hands and invoking Allah: 'O Allah! If You are not angry with me I don't care, but Your grace is more befitting to me. I seek refuge in the light of Your Face, That which has enlightened darkness and on Whom the matters of this life and the Hereafter have settled, that Your Anger does not come on me and that Your Curse does not befall me. To You is our obedience until You are pleased and there is no might or strength except with You.'

The President's Envoy

I was left in my cell for three days, and then taken to the same room as before where I found a tall, blond man sitting. He said: 'Sit down Madam Zainab. We know that the people here have put you through some hardship. Let me introduce myself: I am from the President's office and I'm here to reach an agreement with you. The whole country loves you and we love you too, but you're angry with us and so don't want to reach an agreement with us. I swear, however, that if you do, we'll get you out of this hell-hole today. We all admit that this situation does not suit you. Not only do I promise to get you out of prison but I'm also sanctioned to promise you the post of Minister of Social Affairs once you're released instead of Hikmat Abu Zaid.'

'Did you flog Hikmat Abu Zaid and loose the dogs on her before she became Minister for Social Affairs?'

'What are you saying? Has this happened to you? Here? How can this be when we are in awe simply because of your presence here!'

'What do you want from me?'

'The *Ikhwan* have put all the blame on you. Hudaibi has confused the issue. 'Abd al-Fattah Isma'il and Sayyid Qutb have told us everything. But we feel they're trying to save themselves by incriminating you alone. This is why I came myself today, by orders from President Nasir, so that we can reach an agreement and then you can come out with us. I'll take you home in my car myself. Furthermore, I'd like to inform you that we know from what the *Ikhwan*'s members have said that they wanted to overthrow the government and that it was you who devised the plan to kill Nasir and four of his Ministers. We want you to clarify your position and the roles of al-Hudaibi and Sayyid Qutb in this affair, and the names of the four Ministers whose death you sought. Please speak! Explain the matter in detail!'

'First, the *Ikhwan* did not conspire to overthrow the government. Nor did they plan to kill Nasir nor any ministers, nor anyone else. The matter we concerned ourselves with was the study of Islam and the eradication of Muslims' decadence.'

He stopped me abruptly: 'Madam Zainab! I'm telling you they've told us everything.'

'Could be! But for sure they've said what your butchers wanted them to say. So they said something which did not happen. Again, we were studying Islam, trying to educate a generation that really understands Islam. If this is a crime, then our affair is unto Allah!'

The man swore by Allah that he wanted to help me and that he had come for the sole reason of doing so.

'Thank you. But I have never thought of becoming an employee or a Minister. I have spent all my life in the service of Islam, the issue of the Ministry of Social Affairs doesn't concern me in the least.'

'You could be free. We have offered our help and you have refused it', and with this he left.

I knew a severe beating would follow with only the briefest of respites.

Dear Faces Enter My Cell

The following afternoon, I heard voices that I both knew and loved, the voices of 'Aliyah Hasan al-Hudaibi and Ghadah 'Amar. I tried to look through the flap in my cell door, taking care that no one should notice, but pain overwhelmed all my emotions. I prayed to Allah, begging Him to take my two daughters away from the despots' evil. Blinded with pain, my thoughts were of 'Aliyah, in her last months of pregnancy. How had they dared to arrest her? And Ghadah! What have they done with her baby-girl? Surely, this is the height of cruelty, perversity and savagery. Woe to the people when their rulers are clothed in *Jahiliyyah*. For this *Jahiliyyah* takes hold of all their feelings and wastes their consciences, making them nothing more than butchers. Woe to you Nasir! How much you have deceived your people, you despot!

The cell door opened, and a blanket and pillow were thrown in. Until then, I had spent 18 days sleeping on the bare floor. Two more pillows and blankets were thrust inside. I was stunned. But my astonishment did not last long for the third time my cell door opened, Hamzah al-Basyuni and Safwat escorted in 'Aliyah al-Hudaibi and Ghadah 'Amar. Fortunately, they left us alone. 'Aliyah rushed towards me, taking me in her arms and kissing me. I was distracted from my pain and suffering. She began by asking the craziest of questions: 'Are you *Hajjah* Zainab? Are you really *Hajjah* Zainab?'

I looked at Ghadah, her eyes filled with tears: 'Don't you recognize me?'

'No *Hajjah*! You've changed a lot. You've lost an alarming amount of weight, and your face now looks like that of your brother, Sa'd al-Din.'

'That's only natural. You don't know the horror I'm living in. Besides, I don't eat more than a spoonful of salad a day, which one of the soldiers throws me in fright, lest he's caught feeding me.'

She arranged the blankets and pillows, then sat and asked me for a copy of the Qur'an. Poor 'Aliyah! She thought we were dealing with human beings. She had forgotten we were dealing with the enemies of the Qur'an! Would I expect them to allow me to have one?

Yet amazingly, both Ghadah and 'Aliyah offered me their own small copies of the Qur'an which they had been able to retain. I sat down and, to ease my aching limbs, I stretched my legs. 'Aliyah saw the signs of torture. She asked me about them, so I read: '(*Woe to the makers of the pit (of fire), fire supplied (abundantly) with fuel. Behold! They sat over against the (fire). And they witnessed (all) that they were doing against the believers. And they ill-treated them for no other reason than that they believed in God, Exalted in power, Worthy of all praise).*'[5]

Ghadah began to cry silently. As for 'Aliyah, she could not believe her ears, naively asking for confirmation to the contrary.

'Does this really happen to ladies?'

'Aliyah is a good-hearted woman. It was not her fault

that her imagination could not stretch to the extent of Nasir's butchery. For most people, Nasir's enmity towards Allah and towards the people who call to Him would have been incomprehensible.

The Death of Mustafa al-Nahhas

'Aliyah gently moved me away from the walls of the cell so that she could relate to me the news of Mustafa al-Nahhas Pasha's death. Feelings of faithfulness choked my throat as I prayed for him: 'O Allah! You are able to spare him Your punishment as he is in need of Your Mercy.'

Al-Nahhas had died two or three days after my arrest. At his funeral thousands upon thousands thronged the streets in a huge demonstration. The roads leading to al-Husain Mosque had been blocked and his coffin touched by supporters shouting: 'There is no leader after al-Nahhas.' The slogans and banners carried by the *Ikhwan*'s members on the funeral march were relayed to me as was the attempt by the security forces to halt the demonstration. Nor were the comments of the foreign media forgotten. Our conversation was long and, for me, a comfort to know our work continued. The people had used the occasion of al-Nahhas's death to broadcast their views loud and clear: 'There is no leader after al-Nahhas.' It seemed that by means of this slogan, they were saying: 'Down with all false leaderships! You wear false masks! Your veils have dropped and your lies and deception are revealed! You are drowning in your own delusions, held aloft by your mirage. You are as wooden struts, and the fire of truth will consume you, then you will become ashes which will be sent hither and thither by the wind.'

Some 20,000 demonstrators had been arrested. Indeed, al-Nahhas's funeral had been a call by the righteous, a declaration of their truth. It showed the true colour of

Egypt and the suppressed feelings of its sons and daughters. Mustafa al-Nahhas had been a man who never held a grudge even against his enemies. A man strong enough to admit when he was wrong whenever this was the case. He was truly a national leader.

I asked 'Aliyah whether my brother Saif al-Ghazali, a Wafdist, had been arrested. She could neither confirm nor deny it. Silence reigned for a while, then, she gently tapped me on the shoulder, saying: '*Hajjah*, everything has a decree with Him! [Allah]'

I continued to think about that splendid funeral. It attested to the fact that the *Ummah* was not dead. Forget the media insinuations to the contrary. Forget that the foreign media in particular portrayed Nasir as an upstanding man. What had happened clearly indicated that a time will come when the truth will be discovered and the people will know their rulers for what they really are - rulers who sell their consciences and people by crushing Islam and its followers so as to buy their thrones and trivial luxuries.

I turned towards Ghadah, asking her about her family. With tears in her eyes, she explained that her husband had fled to the Sudan and her mother was ill - torn between her grandchildren - Sumayyah who was ill and Halah who was still suckling. Had it not been for these two, Ghadah added, her mother would not have cared for anything.

I calmed her, prayed for us all and asked about D'ia al-Tubji. Had he married or not? Apparently both he and his bride were arrested on their wedding day, his wife still wearing her wedding dress. Both his sister Muna and his brother, a doctor, were also arrested.

'Maybe they're aiming to arrest everyone and anyone who has had any link with the *Ikhwan*?'

'No, no', intervened 'Aliyah, 'they're arresting anyone seen praying!'

Then, Ghadah began telling me about the savage arrests and the house-to-house searches which went on both day and night.

'In their time neither the Mongols nor the Romans', I said, 'have harmed the Muslims as much as Nasir and his butchers. Nasir's own brand of perversity has made us forget the crimes of all other criminals throughout the entire history of mankind. Nasir is rebellious, shuns the truth, and is blind to the light. No wonder he arrests women and flogs them, no wonder he kills men and orphans children.'

Ghadah looked at me, her gaze resting on my swollen legs and feet: 'Hajjah, I think our turn for torture has arrived! May Allah help us and give us patience. I'll fetch a towel from my suitcase to cover your legs with. Don't you have your own suitcase, Hajjah?'

'My daughter! I've been in these blood-stained clothes for 18 days.'

Ghadah began to cry. She looked at my clothes stained with dry blood and fester and suggested she help me change them. When she lifted them the scars caused by the floggings horrified us both. She was loud in protest and indignation, hardly able to believe such treatment could be dealt out to a woman.

I tried to comfort her and thanked Allah, saying that my suffering was for His sake and not for the sake of some worldly goal. I thanked Allah that He graced us with Islam and honoured us with 'there is no god but Allah and Muhammad is His Messenger.'

'Aliyah tried to comfort me, saying that her sister, Khalidah al-Hudaibi, had said that her arrest would not matter so long as she was put in the same cell as myself. I was very moved by this, but thought that if Khalidah had seen me in this state she would probably change her mind, and I asked Allah to preserve her from such hardship.

So did I ask Allah to preserve all our sisters and brothers from the unjust people and their injustice.

Taking Food - A Form of Worship

Suddenly, when we had stopped talking, the door opened. My gloomy guard brought three pieces of bread and a metal saucer of boiled beans. 'Aliyah took them from him.

I could not stand the smell of the food. And yet 'Aliyah was pregnant and the signs of her exhaustion quite apparent. She brought the food over and, as if sensing my disgust, said: '*Hajjah*, the food is good!'

She gave me one piece of bread and Ghadah another and began to eat her own portion. Ghadah followed.

'I have to eat', 'Aliyah said, 'for the guest who is here', pointing at her stomach.

When they saw that I did not partake, they both stopped eating.

'We eat and we say with each bite 'in the Name of Allah, the Merciful, the Compassionate', braved 'Aliyah.

Still, I could not swallow it, so she carried on: '*Hajjah*! You must have lost more than half your body weight because you are not eating. Eating in such circumstances is akin to worship. Nasir's butchers will be delighted if Zainab al-Ghazali dies as a result. Besides, you know such abstinence is forbidden in Islam.'

I tried, but to no avail, to explain that I ate just enough, and that Allah had enabled me to survive on a spoonful of salad. She was adamant, persisting until I gave in. But Allah knows, though, that was not eating but rather torture.

The following day, I would be able to share with 'Aliyah and Ghadah my daily sight of al-Murshid through the hole in the cell door. I told them of the peace this had brought me. 'Aliyah would now be able to see her father again, if only going daily to the toilet.

For the rest of the day we sat listening to Ghadah telling us of her arrest, and how she had met Hamidah Qutb. I learned that the entire Qutb family had been arrested. Hours passed, ominous and heavy, with nothing to break our suffering save the congregational prayers we performed from time to time.

Nights of Torture and Bargaining

Safwat al-Rubi, accompanied by another soldier, came after *'Isha* prayer and took me back to the same office that I had been in twice before.

There was a man sitting there. I greeted him, but he did not reply, except to say: 'Are you Zainab al-Ghazali?'

'Yes.'

He indicated that I should sit on a chair in front of him.

'So you're Zainab al-Ghazali. Why do you do all this harm to yourself? All this, for the sake of the *Ikhwan*? Each of its members is trying to save himself and throw you, alone, into the well. We feel for you! So this is why I thought it my duty to pull you out. But first I will have to agree with you on a few things. Then you'll be free to go home. Not only this, but I'm also authorized to tell you, on Nasir's behalf, that if you agree with us, and behave reasonably, we'll give you back your Muslim Ladies Headquarters and magazine. We'll also give you a monthly allowance for the magazine of E£2,000, plus substantial financial support to help improve your group further. If you'll agree with a few things I'll send for your clothes and in one hour we'll meet with Nasir. We all feel for you, knowing that it is the *Ikhwan* who has put you through this, may God forgive them. But the President has a big heart!'

I listened in silence, incredulous that they should employ this trick again.

'What do you say Madam Zainab? By Allah! The

President intends to sack Hikmat Abu Zaid and appoint you as Minister in her place. We want you to co-operate with us. Open your heart and tell us everything, then you will know that I am your brother and want only what's good for you. There are also many good people outside who love you and are mediating for you. They're turning the world upside down just for you.'

'I don't want to become a Minister. Such a scenario has never occurred to me before and is not likely to occur now. As for the Muslim Ladies Group and its magazine, I have delegated their matters to Allah. It is not necessary for Muslims to work under the banner of a group or magazine, for we all work under the banner of "there is no god but Allah and Muhammad is His Messenger".'

'So why were you planning to re-organize the *Ikhwan*, Madam Zainab?'

'We are different in our understanding of everything. I, for example, think that the Muslim Ladies Group which I established in 1937 together with its magazine, are not dissolved. But Nasir thinks he dissolved it by confiscating its properties and belongings. Muslims have complete confidence in Allah, and what Allah upholds, human beings cannot dissolve. The *Ikhwan* are the same as the Muslim Ladies Group and the *da'wah* of Allah carries on and the word of truth is upheld forever. Nasir will perish, but the Word of Allah will persist. When our life-terms come to an end, the unjust will surely know what final destiny they are headed for.

'Allah's religion will be upheld, and there will always be a group from the Muslim *Ummah* who will uphold truth, defend our religion, and make *Jihad* for His sake. This group will not be affected by those who oppose them until Allah establishes His Will. I pray to Allah to be from among those who enjoin truth and forbid falsehood, from those who show the *Ummah* its way to Allah. For these are the successors of the Prophet (peace be upon him), and it is the people who will revive this religion.

'The establishment of the *Ikhwan* group was not a haphazard decision by Hasan al-Banna, rather it was the execution of Allah's command. To establish His state and practise His laws. This is why Nasir has no right to dissolve the *Ikhwan*.'

'By Allah, you are an orator. However, I didn't come here to take a lesson from you about the *Ikhwan*. I came to find a solution to the calamity you have got yourself in. The *Ikhwan*'s members have placed all the blame on you. 'Abd al-Fattah Isma'il says that you recruited him. Al-Hudaibi has washed his hands of you and put all the blame on your shoulders. He says you are the one who founded "the secret organization". Sayyid Qutb too blames you. You are either too nice or too crazy for all this. So Nasir wants to save you. Nasir, in whose hands the whole future of the country rests, wants to save you and help you begin afresh. He knows that you are a good orator who has an influence on people, and someone the people love. Indeed your audience is huge.

'Zainab, you really are pathetic for yours is a winning card. Is there anyone else whom Nasir wants to draw so near to him and yet who refuses? Don't mind me saying this but you really are crazy! I say this because I seek only your benefit. Throughout your life, may God prolong it, you have done good deeds and raised orphans. Look, be reasonable *Hajjah* and listen to me!'

'Is what you've said not enough?'

'Tell me a very simple thing and you'll see many good things after it. Give me the names of all the *Ikhwan*'s brothers who used to come to your house and tell me further how they sought to kill Nasir after you'd received orders from al-Hudaibi to do so. We also want to know Sayyid Qutb's stand on this, full details of the plan and how it was elaborated. For my part, I swear by the head of Nasir that if you do tell me everything you will leave prison tonight to start your new job as Social Affairs Minister. This is a golden opportunity, don't waste it! I swear to you by my honour and the President's honour, be reasonable and think properly of your own benefit. All *Ikhwan*'s members think only of themselves.'

At this moment we were interrupted by a huge person, in whose eyes I saw only the devil: 'Colonel', he charged, 'we have all the recordings which we took from her houses in al-Zaitun and Misr al-Jadidah since 1958. If you want, we'll bring them for you to listen to.'

'You can go now Riyad.'

The colonel turned again to me: 'Look Zainab! I know that your husband is a good man, and I want to help you for his sake and yours. Moreover, some of your brothers are dear friends of mine. I want to help you, and the President is keen that you reach an agreement with us. He wants to help you too. I promise you, by my honour and the President's honour, that if we agree, I will burn those tapes here in front of you. We want to pull you out of the mess you have got yourself into. By Allah, we are better Muslims than them. For what is Islam? Islam means that one should not harm his fellow human beings!'

I responded sarcastically: 'What about the things you see here? Does this not harm your fellow human beings?'

'By the Prophet', foolishly said he, 'we are nice people. Just agree with us and you'll see for yourself.'

'I pray to Allah to forgive you and to make you Muslims.'

At this juncture, he picked up a pen and took some papers from his desk drawer: 'Madam Zainab, tell me the names of all the people who used to come to your home.'

'I don't remember, for I don't memorize names and besides I don't ask for names.'

75

'Well, let us leave this issue for now, we'll come back to it later. Let us talk about al-Hudaibi and Sayyid Qutb.'

'On what basis?'

'Their attempt to kill Nasir and take over power.'

'Sir! The issue is greater than the killing of Nasir and the taking over of power. Killing Nasir is a futile issue, one which Muslims are not bothered about. The real issue is the issue of Islam. Islam is currently not upheld. We are working to change this, to establish Islam once again and to educate our Muslim youth for it. If Nasir is fighting against Islam in the name of Muslims and denies the application of *Shari'ah*, claiming it to be leading to backwardness, fanaticism and degradation, then we don't care.'

'You're crazy! What you say is dangerous. Don't you know that if you're killed and buried here no one will know about it. It seems you deserve what you're going through. If I leave you here, you'll be killed within the hour.'

'Allah does what He wills and chooses.'

When the colonel heard these words, he turned into a raging monster. He was hysterical, swearing, cursing and gyrating. He called Riyad Ibrahim.

'Leave the tapes to the courts, she's crazy. Deal with her as you will and call Sa'id to assist you.' 500 lashes were my punishment.

Sa'id began by hitting me on my hands, feet, back, all over my body. He would leave me facing the wall for about an hour after a session and then return to deliver more. Then they brought in a group of Muslim brothers and began whipping them, while asking them all the while to swear the most disgusting curses at me. The brothers refused and the round of torture increased. Among those beaten in this way was Pilot D'ia al-Tubji who, you will remember, was arrested on his wedding day.

Now Hamzah al-Basyuni's Turn

Then it was the turn of Hamzah al-Basyuni. The pain had become unbearable and al-Basyuni was now accompanied by Riyad, who screamed at me: 'Woman! Be reasonable and think about yourself. We only want to end your suffering. Advise her Hamzah!'

'Are you going to confess as all the men have or not?'

'I don't have anything to confess. The only thing we gathered together for was the reviving of the 'aqidah of Tawhid in the hearts of our youth.'

Hamzah turned to Safwat who was behind him and asked him to bring two chairs, one for him and another for me. He carried on: 'Her husband is a friend of mine, this is why I'm persisting with her.'

When the chair was brought, and Hamzah asked me to sit I was unable to do so, my whole body wreaked with pain. He asked me once more to sit, so I told him that I could not and that he must speak with me while I stood.

'You are the one who has made yourself go through all this and degraded yourself to this point', he railed. 'You have become very ugly and your legs look like those of a savage. Your husband will be grieved when he sees you like this. You look 60 years of age. Your husband is a friend of mine and I feel for him. Look at your hands, they look like a builder's hands!'

At that Safwat said: 'What are you saying Sir? She looks 120 years old. Her face is ugly. I bet her husband will curse her and swear and the divorce decree will reach her through the post.'

I did not respond. Rather, I looked at both men with contempt and disgust. I do not know if they felt the contempt in my looks or were stupid enough not to notice it. Yes, they seemed stupid to me, cowards, like dirt-stained flies. They thought they were frightening me, but I felt sure it was they who were afraid of me.

Al-Basyuni shouted to Safwat to put me facing the wall, but I rushed there myself before he could do so and raised my hands in readiness. Safwat flogged me again while another soldier brought a container full of boiling oil and put a number of whips into it.

Hamzah and Safwat then left, leaving me with that wretched Sa'id who forced me to watch as he dipped whips into the boiling oil. Shortly after, about ten soldiers came into the room; they each took a whip and began beating the floor and shouting at me: 'B........, we're sharpening these for you!'

I did not look at them, for I was busy in the remembrance of Allah. I recited the verse: (*Men said to them: 'A great army is gathering against you': and frightened them, but it (only) increased their faith: they said: 'For us Allah suffices and He is the best Disposer of affairs*).'[6] Then came the butcher al-Rubi, ordering the soldiers out. They had postponed my killing for that night at least. He dragged me by the arm back to my cell.

Back to the Cell

Although 'Aliyah and Ghadah had been asleep, they woke the minute I returned. Concerned about the blood pouring from my feet, 'Aliyah inquired what they had done to me. I praised Allah, and asked her to go back to sleep. I repeated the Prophet's saying: 'In the Name of Allah, I seek refuge in Allah's Might and Omnipotence from the evil I face and fear.'

For two days in this state, although I was paralyzed with pain, I tried not to show how much I was suffering out of pity for 'Aliyah and Ghadah. They made a point of not asking me about that dreadful night. The signs of my torture had been enough for them.

Another Night Falls

The cell door opened after *'Isha* prayer.

'You woman, Zainab, stand up!'

Safwat pulled me forward by my hands. I lost my balance and almost fell because I was so exhausted. I was led into a small room, and left alone briefly whilst Safwat fetched a new inquisitor: 'Who are you woman?'

'Zainab al-Ghazali al-Jubaili.'

'Why are you here?'

'I don't know.'

'You must know! You're here because you, al-Hudaibi, Sayyid Qutb and 'Abd al-Fattah Isma'il conspired to kill Nasir.'

'Such a conspiracy never took place.'

'Be careful what you say, for today there will be killing and not just floggings. Do you know who I am? I'm what they call the Military prison's monster! Do you understand?'

'There is here none except dogs and beasts. Since I came here, I have not seen, if we exclude all those oppressed Muslim brothers, a single human being.'

Hearing this, he kicked me and then pushed me to the floor. Then he repeatedly stood on me and then harangued me against the wall: 'We don't want this sophistry, be sensible and talk!', and he hit me with both hands on the face.

Safwat made me sit down on a chair, left the room and locked the door behind him. A short while later, another man came in: 'Zainab! What are you doing to yourself? You're cursing people and making fun of them. The President has a big heart and wants to help you. We just want you as a witness in this case and then we'll get you out of the crime the *Ikhwan* has got you into.'

'The Muslim Brothers have committed no crime. The only crime is that scoundrels like you are ruling this good country!'

'You're psychologically disturbed, you are, woman. I'll send someone who knows how to deal with you.'

He left, and I thanked Allah that he did not ask me to stand up, for I was exhausted. A number of violent visitors ensued, each with their own peculiar brand of perversity and persuasive measures. More claims of how Nasir, himself, wanted to help me. How if I agreed to confess to the court the crimes of the *Ikhwan*, I would be freed. How they wanted to help me, if only for the sake of my husband. More floggings and worse if I refused. Finally, I was allowed back to my cell, to be given time to rest and come back to my senses - to give them the answer they wanted the next day.

A Short Break

I tried to sleep but could not. After *Fajr* prayer, Ghadah asked me what had happened. I responded: 'I ask Allah to hold our steps firm in following the truth. They want to put me through a test. They are asking for the impossible.'

'May Allah help you!'

Ghadah wanted to know more but I did not respond. I was tired and had to prepare myself for the forthcoming meeting. 'Aliyah understood this, and silenced Ghadah. So the remainder of that night and the following day passed peacefully.

The Deadly Night!

Back to the venue of torture with Safwat and this time a man that I had not seen before. He ordered Safwat to leave and asked me to sit on a chair near the desk.

'Madam Zainab, you have tired the people who want to help you. Today it is me who has come to help and I hope God will help me and guide me so that you change your stand on the *Ikhwan*, for it is enough that they have put you in this embarrassing position. You are deceived by them, you think they really want Islam, yet all they want is power for themselves.'

Like those before him, he repeated the offers, inducements, amplifications of integrity and the like. His story was the same: if I agreed to act as an approver of the state's case against the *Ikhwan*, I would walk free. All that I cherished would be restored, and personal glory in the shape of a Ministerial post would be mine.

I was offered coffee but declined. Reminded that Hudaibi and Sayyid Qutb had laid the blame for the *Ikhwan*'s crimes at my door, or so they said, finally, I was left with pen and paper. My testimony was to give them the final proof they needed about the *Ikhwan*'s interest. Instead, I wrote only of that which I knew to be true:

> . . . We gathered with the youth of the *Ikhwan* to study books of *Fiqh*, *Sunnah*, *Hadith* and *Tafsir*. We were studying Ibn Hazm's *Muhalla*, Ibn al-Qayyim's *Zad al-Ma'ad*, al-Mundhiri's *al-Targhib wa al-Tarhib*, Sayyid Qutb's *Fi zilal al-Qur'an* and extracts from Qutb's *Ma'alim Fi al-Tariq*. We studied the *Sunnah* of the Prophet and his Companions and the way in which *da'wah* was established. All this was with the permission and guidance of al-Hudaibi. The aim of all these studies was to form sound guidance for our Muslim youth such that we may bring back Islam's glory and establish God's *din* on earth.

After much reflection we decided to re-organize the *Ikhwan* in all its aspects as a means of facilitating our aims for this *Ummah*'s youth, a youth which is lost within this *Jahili* society. We anticipated this work would go on for 13 years after which we would make a survey throughout the country. If at that time less than 75% of the population believed in Islam as a way of life, then we would prolong the period of education and study for another 13 years, and so on and so forth, until at least 75% of the whole population were firm for Islam. What is Nasir so scared of? By our call for the establishment of an Islamic state? What are his lieutenants so scared of? Perhaps generations will perish before what we want is realized, so what are you so afraid of? Killing Nasir is not, and never has been, one of our considerations. It simply does not figure in our cause. The equation is much larger than you credit. Besides, killing is anathema for true Muslims, yet you persist in using it as an excuse to murder us believers. Tell me, who asked you to torture and execute us? Is it Zionism? Is it Communism?

What makes atheistic Communism, and a deviated West which has rejected Christianity, as well as the terrorism of International Zionism tremble? I'll tell you. It's the return of Islam with its beliefs, laws and ways of dealing with people. Yes! Islam's return frightens all these different groupings. This is why they spy on us and order their agents to finish us off. But Allah will establish His light and will curse the disbelievers. You can kill us today, but others like us, also holding the banner of Islam, will follow. As for the Muslim Ladies' magazine, the Muslim Ladies Group, indeed the whole world, we reject them all if they come to us by any other means than for Allah. We only want Allah, His way and His *Shari'ah*.

Zainab al-Ghazali al-Jubaili.

Safwat al-Rubi came to collect what I had written. A while later, the man who had asked me to write them came back holding some papers - which were not the ones I had written; these he tore up, throwing them in disgust in my face. The aim: to make me think he had destroyed my originals.

'She deserves to be executed', he bellowed at Safwat. 'I wanted to help her, but she refuses my extended hand. Let them hang her as agreed.' With this he left.

More ferocious beating and kicking from Safwat ensued before yet again I was hurled back into my cell. I was perplexed, for if, as they said, the case was clear and all its elements had been discovered, why, then had they not put me on trial? If it really were as they said, there would be no point to the continuous tide of torture and temptation. Or did they somehow enjoy consigning me to a slow death following some pre-designed plan?

A Letter from Nasir

Once the cell door was locked, I entered another world. Exhaustion, fatigue, starvation and pain had left deep marks on both my soul and body. The psychological abuse I had suffered was becoming almost as intolerable and unbearable as their physical perversions. Like a fire raging uncontrollably, my every move seemed to add fuel to the devastation already reaped by others.

My only comfort was the *Adhan* of *Fajr* which I could hear coming from the outside. And from 'Aliyah, a tranquillizer the doctor had given her. I took the pill hoping to find some solace in sleep and an inner peace in my prayers to Allah.

I woke to find Ghadah reminding me that today was the 8th October. May Allah make it pass well for us all.

Just before noon, the cell door opened. It was Safwat, accompanied by two soldiers carrying a large suitcase. I immediately recognized it as mine.

'Zainab, these are the clothes that we asked for you from your home.'

83

Safwat began taking the clothes out of the suitcase, and then, put them back in and locked it.

'Who asked for all these clothes, and who brought them?', I asked.

'We decided it and your sister Hayat brought them.'

As quickly as Safwat and the soldiers had arrived, they left. I closed my eyes and passed out. 'Aliyah and Ghadah rushed over to me and tried to revive me by massaging my hands and feet.

'*Hajjah*, the issue is simple. They thought you needed clothes, so they brought some for you. The whole thing is that straightforward.'

'No 'Aliyah, it's a calamity!'

'Why *Hajjah*? They saw your clothes were torn and that you needed others.'

'No! No! 'Aliyah, this is a test! Why bring clothes for me only? I'm uneasy about all this. It can only mean another test, and this of greater magnitude than the previous ones.'

I began asking Allah to hold my steps firm in following the truth. We prayed '*Asr*, and, as we were in the fourth *rak'ah*, Safwat al-Rubi came in and harshly pulled me to my feet. He took me to the end of the corridor, and left me in a dark, stinking cell which was full of mice.

Frightened, I sat down, my body shaking from the cold. The darkness of the cell increased my fear. I sought Allah's help in overcoming it all (. . . *for without doubt, in the remembrance of Allah do hearts find satisfaction*).[7]

Suddenly the lights were switched on, and Safwat came in, thrusting a piece of paper at me: 'Read this letter!'

I looked at the letter and saw written at the top 'The Office of the President'.

By orders of President Jamal 'Abd al-Nasir, Zainab al-Ghazali al-Jubaili is to be tortured more harshly than men.

The letter was signed by Nasir, the President of the Republic and bore the stamp of the state Presidency.

'Allah is Greater than all of you. We have Allah with us', I said to Safwat.

He glared at me with all the ferocity he could muster and mouthed a barrage of foul abuse. When I did not respond, he left, only to return with al-Basyuni.

I was forced to read Nasir's letter again and, having done so, I threw it to the floor.

'Our Lord is greater than you perverts. Get out of here you disbelievers!'

'We'll give you one more hour and this is your last chance', smirked al-Basyuni. 'These are your clothes. Think carefully about it for your own sake. The solution to your problem is in your own hands. I advise you to get changed and prepare yourself to meet Field Marshal 'Amir and the President.'

They left, locking the cell door behind them. I began asking Allah for His forgiveness and to give me strength to stand firm in following the truth.

They were back within the hour.

'You haven't changed your clothes? Do you want to die?' Al-Basyuni seemed incredulous. 'All right! You've sold yourself. Safwat! Take this B.......! She sees herself as redemption for Sayyid Qutb and al-Hudaibi . . . For they want rid of her and claim their innocence.'

Safwat dragged me violently from the cell and down the long, stench-filled corridor. As I passed my own cell I shouted: 'Allah is Greater' such that Ghadah and 'Aliyah could hear me, for I thought this was really my end as Hamzah al-Basyuni had said.

Notes and References

1. Ibn Hisham: *Al-Sirah al-Nabawiyyah*, Vol.I, p.342, Dar al-Qalam edition, Beirut, Lebanon.

2. *Jahiliyyah* denotes the historical phase before the advent of Islam, but also implies the state of ignorance which marks this phase. The term became, in the Islamic movement's literature, and especially in Sayyid Qutb's writings, a general term for the refusal to adhere fully and completely to the *Shari'ah* in all aspects of life: individual, political, social and economic.

3. Al-Bukhari, *Zakah*.

4. *Al 'Imran*: 139-40.

5. *Al-Buruj*: 4-8.

6. *Al 'Imran*: 173.

7. *Al-Ra'd*: 28.

CHAPTER 4

In the Company of Shams Badran

Safwat marched me up to an officer called Hani who, in turn, took me to Shams Badran's office. Shams Badran's name and atrocities are forever planted in my mind.

He was worse than a beast, a man alien to all human norms and manners. More ferocious than any from the wild animal kingdom. His was a legend of unsurpassable cruelty and torture. His delight and pleasure was to inflict pain and suffering. His one aim: to get Muslims to abandon their religion. He was not to succeed. That villain of villains underestimated our strength, underestimated our faith in Allah, and forgot the power of His guidance.

'So you're Zainab al-Ghazali?', he arrogantly postulated.

'Yes.'

'Woman mind yourself and speak reasonably and see where your benefit lies. Let's finish our investigation with you, so that we can deal with somebody else. Or else, I swear by the might of Nasir that I will tear you apart with my whips.'

'Allah does what He wills and chooses!'

'What is this strange gibberish, you B..........!'

I did not respond.

'What's your relationship with Hasan al-Hudaibi?'

87

'Brotherhood in Islam.'

'What Brotherhood?'

'Brotherhood in Islam.'

'What is Sayyid Qutb's profession?'

'The Professor, *Imam* Sayyid Qutb is a *Mujahid* in the name of Allah and an exegete of the Qur'an, leader, reviver of Islam and *Mujtahid*.'

'What does all this mean?'

I answered him again; stressing each word, I pronounced: 'Professor Sayyid Qutb is a leader, reformer, Islamic writer, nay, he is the greatest of Islamic writers [of modern times] and true inheritor of Prophet Muhammad (peace be upon him).'

In response to a simple gesture with his finger, his butchers began beating me violently.

'What did you say, madam?'

I did not answer, so he carried on: 'And what is al-Hudaibi's profession?'

'Professor *Imam* al-Hudaibi is a sworn-in *Imam* who belongs to the *Ikhwan*. He is committed to the commandments of Allah and he struggles for the sake of Allah until the whole Muslim *Ummah* returns to Allah's Book and the *Sunnah* of His Prophet (peace be upon him).'

No sooner had I finished than his butchers struck once more.

'Nonsense! What are you saying you B........?'

At this point, Hasan Khalil intervened: 'Leave her Pasha,[1] there is an important point I'd like to address.'

He came forward and held me by the arm, saying: 'Have you read Sayyid Qutb's *Ma'alim fi al-Tariq*?'

'Yes, I have.'

A man sitting in the room, for many soldiers would come now and then to assist in the investigation and to increase the pressure on me, chirped up: 'Could you give us a brief summary of this book?'

'In the Name of Allah, the Merciful, the Compassionate. Peace and blessings be on our master Muhammad and his family and Companions.'

'B........! Do you think you are standing on a mosque's *minbar*? We are not in a church you children of ....' Shams Badran's insolence was all too clear.

Hasan Khalil intervened: 'Pasha, she is to be excused. Carry on Zainab, what did you understand from the book?'

'Sayyid Qutb's *Ma'alim* calls upon Muslims to review themselves according to the Qur'an and the *Sunnah* of the Prophet, and correct their conceptions *vis-à-vis* the *'aqidah* of *Tawhid*. If Muslims find themselves - as is the case today - disconnected from Allah's Book and His Prophet's *Sunnah*, they should rush for repentance and return to their Lord and the Prophet. Sayyid Qutb also calls upon Muslims to completely disassociate themselves from the prevailing *Jahiliyyah*. If the *Ummah* goes back to Allah's Book, His aims and goals and is committed to His religion, then its *'aqidah* is right. Sayyid Qutb believes in the necessity of enlightening the *Ummah* by reviewing its *'aqidah*. Only then can this *Ummah* truly decide, from the bottom of its heart and conscience, that it is committed to assume the implications of "there is no god but Allah and Muhammad is His Messenger".'

Silence followed for a while, and then Hasan Khalil sarcastically exclaimed: 'She is one hell of an orator!'

'A writer too!', added another.

He took out a set of the Muslim Ladies' magazine, ones that had been confiscated when they raided my home. He began reading a few lines from one of my editorials. He was interrupted by Shams Badran: 'I didn't understand a word of what she said.'

And, as his butchers resumed their flogging: 'Clarify what you said, you B........!'

Hasan Khalil again intervened, as if setting a trap for me: 'It's alright Pasha; a little more time please. I want to understand the implications of "there is no god but Allah and Muhammad is His Messenger".'

'Muhammad (peace be upon him) has come to take humanity out of the worship of human beings and idols to the worship of Allah alone. This is the meaning of "there is no god but Allah". "Muhammad is His slave and Messenger", means that what the Prophet (peace be upon him) has brought as revelation, i.e. the Qur'an and the authentic *Sunnah*, is the truth which is obligatory on us all. It is for us to implement at both the practical as well as conceptual levels. And this is the sound conception of the *Shahadah*.'

'Enough stupidity!', shouted Shams Badran, signalling for the flogging to recommence.

Again Hasan Khalil, as if he was holding the rope around my neck, acted as interlocutor: 'Do me a favour Pasha, just a few moments more.'

He turned towards me, asking: 'Are we Muslims or *Kafirs*?'

'Subject yourself critically to the Qur'an and the *Sunnah*, and you will know where you stand *apropos* Islam.'

'You B.......!'

The venom in Shams Badran's voice was only the beginning of his garbaged diatribe. 'Suspend her in the air, this beating's of no use!', he said.

A thick iron bar and two wooden bases, the instrument on which they would hang me, was prepared.

'Please give me trousers . . . . I beg you!'

Hasan Khalil agreed and a soldier returned with a pair so quickly you would have thought he had taken his own off. I was escorted to an adjacent room to change.

'Five hundred floggings!', shouted Shams Badran, the great battlefield hero, as my hands and feet were tied.

His whips found every part of my body, the cruellest thing that *Jahiliyyah* had known both in terms of cruelty and bestiality. As the torture and pain intensified, I could

not suppress my screams any longer; I raised my voice
to Allah. I repeated His great Name: 'O Allah! O Allah!'
Whilst the whips tore into my body, my heart found
contentment and affinity with Allah. I lost consciousness
but they tried to arouse me to take more punishment.
Blood poured from my feet, and unable to pull myself
up, I tried to lean on the wall. Safwat persisted with his
whip. I begged to be allowed to sit on the floor but
Shams Badran shouted: 'No! No! Where is your God
now? Call Him to save you from my hands! Yet call
Nasir and you'll see what will happen! Answer me, where
is your God?'

'Answer me, you B.........!'

My voice, faint with exhaustion, was barely audible:
'Allah, may He be exalted, the Doer, the Mighty, the
Firm.'

The Cell of Water

That brutal session over, Safwat's butchers began
pushing me out of Badran's office towards my cell. But
we had only taken a few steps when Hasan Khalil called:
'Come back Safwat, the Pasha wants Zainab again.'

To my surprise, by the time we had returned to Badran's
office, Hamidah Qutb was also there. I recognized her
immediately but by now my features were very much
changed and she was clearly unsure as to my identity.

Shams Badran asked my respected daughter Hamidah:
'Is this Zainab al-Ghazali?'

At that, she scrutinized my features closely, and only
then responded in the affirmative.

Exhausted, I was unable to follow the line of questioning
that Shams Badran pursued with Hamidah. All I could
gather was his asking about Fatimah 'Isa, a sister in the
cell in front of mine. As Hamidah began her answers, I

was ordered out of the room. Outside I collapsed in a heap on the floor. Safwat ordered one of his soldiers to call 'Abd al-Ma'bud, the nurse. When he arrived, he woke me with smelling salts. Immediately, I was commanded to stand, then to walk, the whips all the time hastening my steps. I fell repeatedly only to be dragged back up and forced on. God! Was this man or beast at work?

I heard a voice shout: 'Take her to Room 5.'

'Take her to the cell of water', another interposed.

I was taken to a room and ordered to sit on the floor while 'Abd al-Ma'bud treated my wounds. Then the cell door opened. I saw behind it an iron dam more than a metre wide. I was ordered to take my clothes off and get into the water. I was so petrified, I could not move a muscle.

I concentrated all my attention on the well behind the dam, and with as much strength as I could muster, told Safwat: 'I will never take my clothes off!'

'You will go into the water in one dress only.'

'I am wearing one dress only.'

'Then I'll tear it up for you!', and with this he slashed at my miserable garb.

'Take off your trousers, you B.........! It's a waste to leave them on since you're going to die in an hour anyway.'

'Go into the other room then I'll give them to you!'

'What room you B.........! I'll throw you down that well now and get rid of you.'

'At least turn to the side so I can take my trousers off.'

This done, I stood in my torn dress not knowing what to do, until Safwat ordered me to jump in the water. I refused, saying: 'I'll never throw myself in that water. If you want to kill me, then you have to do it yourselves. I will never commit suicide.'

I continued to resist despite their pushing. Eventually Safwat and the two soldiers threw me in.

I opened my eyes to find myself standing on solid ground. What I had mistaken for a well was actually a cell of water. I sought comfort in Allah: 'In Your Name Lord I submit to You. I am Your slave in all my affairs, and I am on Your Covenant to the best of my ability. Clothe me with the garment of Your Love and shower Your Patience on me, O Allah!'

'Sit down B..........!', railed Safwat.

'How am I going to sit in this water? It's impossible!'

'Sit as you sit in prayer. You know that well enough. Show us your talents and sit down. You've seen nothing yet! Only Nasir knows how to deal with the *Ikhwan*. Go on sit down you B.......!'

The water reached up to my chin.

'Don't move even a single muscle! Nasir has ordered that you be flogged a thousand times a day. And I, I have my own pricing. For here each movement will cost you ten floggings.'

Terrified, I forgot about my torn feet. I forgot my whole being, despite the havoc the water played with my wounds. Had it not been for Allah's Care I would not have been able to endure it. I closed my eyes hoping to distract myself from the pain.

'Pretty! Know that you'll be woken by the whip if you sleep. Here, you only sit. You sit like that. Do you see that hole in the door? That's for watching you from. If you stand, sleep, stretch your hands or your legs, we will flog you. We've put you in the middle of the room, so be careful not to lean with your head on the wall. Dare you do that, and we'll flog you ten times more. If you stand that's ten more. If you stretch your legs or your arms it's five. So call on Hudaibi or Qutb to help you now, you are here in Nasir's hell. If you say "O God!" nobody will help you, but if you say: "O Nasir!", then the gates of Paradise will open to you. Nasir's Paradise. Do you understand?

'Beautiful! There's a lot ahead of you and what is to come will get worse and worse. So be reasonable. I'm ready to beg on your behalf to the Pasha if only you'll tell him all that he wants to know. Are you mad? For whose sake are you doing all this to yourself? Is it for the *Ikhwan*? They've all confessed everything, no thought of sparing you. They've all turned their guns on you.'

I remained silent, though the way I looked at him said it all. Alas, Safwat was a stupid, ignorant animal and could only continue his foolishness.

'Listen to me and save yourself, or you'll be dead by morning!'

Silence.

'Answer me B.........! The matter is simple, I'll take you to his eminence Shams Badran now and you can tell him how Sayyid Qutb and al-Hudaibi agreed to kill Nasir.'

With all my remaining strength I shouted: 'All the brothers are innocent and Allah will take revenge on you. Our goal is not this life, we only seek Allah's pleasure and let whatever happens happen!'

His whip poured down upon me for more than half an hour.

'B.........! You know the instructions and the pricing.'

But I could not sustain my posture, for no one, regardless of their strength, could sit in that manner without moving, for it was sheer pain and torture. Better to be flogged, for the fire of the whip is less painful than that which the water required me to bear. I began thinking about how I could move. If I stretched my legs, water would reach my mouth. So I had to stand and endure the penalty. I delegated the matter to Allah and stood up.

It appeared that the soldiers were sleeping. In any case, I heard the *Adhan* of *Fajr*, so I performed *tayammum*, for the water was filthy and not suitable for *wudu'*. I said the *sunnah* prayer, then the obligatory prayer. At that point the soldiers rushed into the cell and their beatings further lacerated my body. So, I sat back as I was, and the door closed.

'Allah is Sufficient unto us and He is the best Disposer of affairs', I repeated over and over again.

Sambo returned no less than five times to deliver more punishment because I dared to move my position. The villainy of it all!

The Crime

By noon, I had been moved to an adjacent cell. Left alone, I rolled myself in a corner using the wall as a support. That wall was to me like a soft pillow stuffed with ostrich feathers! My pain was excruciating and hunger minced my intestines.

What comfort I found soon dispelled with Safwat's repeated lashings of the wall and floor with his whip, his ardour recharged. He had brought another of his mad dogs along with him, this time to commit the most abominable crime that any human being can commit.

'If you face any resistance from her, use the whip!'

I beseeched Allah: 'O Allah! I am Your slave-girl, following Your path as much as I am able. I am calling You out of my weakness, despondency and inability to drive away the sins of these evil-doers. Protect me with Your Might, and help me surmount their injustice.'

I was awakened from my invocation by the voice of the surly brute who had been brought to rape me: 'Aunty!', he called. I looked at him in amazement. His countenance had changed, resembling more that of a human being's.

'Don't be scared Aunty! I won't hurt you even if they tear me apart.'

'May Allah guide you my son. May Allah bestow His bounties on you!'

The cell door opened violently and Safwat leapt on the man, beating and cursing him: 'You accursed dog! Now you've exposed yourself to the death penalty. Either get on with this job or it is a military court for you. I'll be back in an hour to see what you've done. Save yourself, obey my orders.'

'Yes Sir.'

'O Allah!', I called. 'This is Your mission and we are its soldiers and martyrs. Protect Your soldiers and their honour. Make us stronger than their injustice and torture.'

I was also praying to Allah to guide this man. I had expected after the brutal reminder of his orders that he would be scared and turn into the monster they hoped for. But he was kindly and courageous.

'Why are they torturing you like this Aunty?', he asked with the innocence of a child.

'My son, we are calling people to Allah and want Islam's rule for this country. Don't misunderstand, for we don't want power for ourselves.'

I heard the *Adhan* of *Zuhr*, and made *tayammum* on the wall and prayed. The man asked me to pray for him, so I did. When I stood up to pray the *sunnah*, he said: 'Pray to Allah to help me begin my prayers, Aunty. You are good people, may the wrath of Allah be on you Nasir!'

'Do you know how to make *wudu'*?'

'Of course. I used to persevere in performing prayer, but had the army found out about it, I would have been jailed.'

'Pray, even if they jail you, my son.'

'I will', he said, the light of *iman* shining in his face.

At this juncture a soldier banged violently on the cell door. 'You son of a dog!', he shouted. 'What are you doing?'

'The lady has not finished praying yet.'

'Safwat is coming, he sent me to see what you've done.'

Safwat charged in like a rabid dog. He attacked my young saviour with the utmost savagery, hitting him until he no longer even groaned. Finally they picked him up and took him out. I was left alone to reflect on the suffering this young man would endure on my behalf. Allah had illuminated his heart such that he could not obey the unjust.

Back to the Cell of Water

At sunset, the butchers of the Military prison became active. Their wheels of torture began to roll. During the night they took me back to the cell of water. My intestines screamed with hunger, my throat was cracked from thirst, my bodily wounds scorched my soul. Miraculously, I fell asleep and enjoyed the most beautiful of dreams. Beautiful people wore beautiful clothes made from black silk, adorned with pearls sewn together in gold-embroidered velvet. They carried plates of gold and silver full to the brim with meats and fruits that I had never seen the like of before. I began eating, first from this plate, then another and another. As I awoke I realized I was no longer hungry. or thirsty. Rather, the taste of the food I had eaten in my dream remained in my mouth. I thanked Allah and praised Him for His bounty.

I remained in the pit of water all night until noon the following day when Safwat came. He rolled up his trousers, got into the water and shook me violently: 'For how long are you going to persist in your obstinacy? Save yourself and let us finish with you. Tell us how Sayyid Qutb and al-Hudaibi agreed to kill Nasir. When did they ask you to order 'Abd al-Fattah Isma'il to kill Nasir?'

'None of this happened.'

He left the cell with his usual swearing and cursing, returning nearly an hour later. Dragged out of the water,

I was again placed in the adjacent cell and Safwat left. I trembled, for all my thoughts focused on what happened in this same cell the previous day. I asked Allah, with all the *iman* I had, to preserve me from their plans. Safwat was back within minutes with another officer, called Ibrahim, and told me: 'B........! This officer will speak with you.'

'You can go now, Safwat', his superior commanded.

'Now Madam Zainab, is it not better for you to consider your own interests and work towards that only? These people don't have any god to fear! Have they told you what they did to that soldier who disobeyed his orders yesterday? They shot him dead. Today they're preparing a team of hardened criminals for you. Do what they ask you to do and save yourself. Hasan al-Hudaibi, Sayyid Qutb and 'Abd al-Fattah Isma'il are men who can assume responsibility for what they have done.'

I kept quiet, for I had grown bored of their temptations, bargaining and threats. Besides, I did not think it possible to be tortured more than I had been already.

The officer, as if ashamed for failing in his mission, shouted out to Safwat: 'Do whatever you like with her, she's asked for it.'

Safwat entered, screaming: 'Nasir has sent devils from the Nubah who will devour you. Where are you going to run to now? Every minute that goes by brings you nearer to your end!'

He then left and closed the door behind him.

After '*Asr*, I was again taken to the cell of water where I stayed all night. Just before noon on the fourth day, Safwat came alone and threw me back into the adjacent room. Then, after '*Asr*, back to the cell of water where I stayed until the following day. Day in day out, this same routine ensued until I completely lost track of time and my senses became numbed.

Death to the Beast!

Again, I was taken from the cell of water to the adjacent room.

'What's going to happen to you today has not happened to a mangy dog in a windmill!', roared Safwat to the tune of his whips.

He returned a few moments later with Hamzah al-Basyuni, and a number of dishevelled looking soldiers. Hamzah said:

'You B........! Save yourself and confess everything. Al-Hudaibi, Sayyid Qutb and 'Abd al-Fattah Isma'il have confessed everything. We know from them that Hudaibi asked you to inform 'Abd al-Fattah Isma'il that shedding Nasir's blood is licit because he is a *kafir*. Every one of them has spoken and saved themselves but you persist in wasting yourself.'

Turning to Safwat, he commanded: 'Execute the orders, Safwat! And if any of these dogs disobeys refer him immediately to my office.'

Safwat began explaining to the soldiers what they had to do, in the most despicable, pornographic manner, all vestiges of decency removed. Pointing to one of them, he took unashamed pleasure in his instruction: 'Execute the instruction, you dog! And when you've finished call your friend to do the same. Understood!'

He then left the room and locked the door.

The soldier began begging me to tell them all they needed to know, for he had no wish to hurt me. But if he did not obey orders then a great harm would befall him. With all the strength I could muster, I warned him: 'Come near me, just one step, and I'll kill you. Kill you, understand?'

I could see the man was reluctant but still he moved towards me. Before I knew it, my hands were firmly around his neck. '*Bismillah, Allahu Akbar*', I shouted, and sank my teeth into the side of his neck. The man slipped out of my hands, white foam, like murky soap suds, frothed from his mouth. He fell to the ground motionless. Hardly able to believe what had happened, I slunk backwards, what little strength I had now diluted. For now, at least, I was safe. Allah, the Exalted, had infused in me a strange force. A force sufficient to overcome this beast.

It was a fierce battle in which virtue had beaten depravity. A sign of truth and glad tiding for the sincere, praise be to Allah, 'there is no god but Allah'. All despots run scared, convinced of the efficacy of brute force. Whilst the holders of the message are behind bars, devoid of anything except faith in Allah. The believers' firmness in holding to the truth is something that their oppressors, who have neglected their faith, cannot comprehend.

O my God! How generous are You! How vast is Your Gift! You are our Lord and the Lord of everything! Those who follow Allah's commandments are fought and resisted, but the final abode is always to the righteous!

The cell door opened and Hamzah and Safwat, and their motley crew stood confounded by what they saw: their compatriot gurgling on the ground. They looked, on silently in disbelief. (. . . *Thus was he confounded who (in arrogance) rejected faith* . . .)[2]

They carried the soldier's body away between them. Then the cell of water was again my destiny.

From Mice to Water and Vice Versa

I remained in the cell of water until, at noon of the sixth day, I was again moved to the adjacent room. My nerves were on edge, anticipating what might happen next, for I had gone through every conceivable kind of torture in that place.

I delegated my affairs to Allah and sat leaning against the wall. I sensed something move and, lifting my head saw a continuous stream of mice pouring through the window as if being emptied from a sack.

I was horrified and began trembling uncontrollably. I began repeating: 'I seek refuge in Allah from malice and malicious things. O Allah! Clear away from me iniquity with whatever thing You want and in whatever manner You like!'

I repeated this *du'a* until I heard the *Adhan* of *Zuhr*. I made *tayammum* and prayed. I continued to invoke Allah until the *'Asr* prayer. But no sooner had I finished than the beast Safwat al-Rubi came in. Miraculously, by then nearly all the mice had vanished from my cell, making their escape by the window. Safwat's astonishment was apparent as he scoured every corner of the cell for evidence. A thousand questions manifested on his face.

Unable to digest what he saw, he began cursing and swearing in disappointment. Nothing to do now but return me to the cell of water.

There I remained for eight days, enduring almost unbearable exhaustion and fatigue. On the ninth day, Safwat, Riyad and a soldier in military uniform came to my cell and threatened that this was my last chance to save myself. Again, either I confessed to everything they wanted me to or they would get rid of me.

'Do you really think that your God has a Hell? Hell is here with Nasir! Nasir's Paradise is a real and existing Paradise. Not an imaginative, unreal Paradise like the one that your God promises you!', thundered Riyad.

I continued my silent prayers to Allah, despite the arrival of Hamzah and another ten soldiers.

'Pasha, what shall we do with this B.........?', Safwat asked Hamzah.

Turning to his soldiers, Hamzah seemed sure.

'What did you drink?', he bellowed.

'Tea your Eminence.'

'Tea you dogs! Safwat! Take them away and give each a bottle of wine and a lump of hashish. Feed them everything they want to eat and then throw this B........ to them. I'll give each a reward for his services.'

With that they all left.

I remained in the cell until 'Asr prayer. I was in prayer when the door opened and Safwat rushed towards me, pulling me up savagely by the arm. But it was Riyad who spoke: 'Is it that you want to be a saint? Those soldiers we brought to you are now in hospital, suffering from poisoning. They'll be back tomorrow to devour your flesh. This is Nasir's order, for he'll never leave you alone. We've tried time and again but you refuse to change your position. Do you want to be a martyr? Answer me! Answer me! Where is your whip Safwat?'

Safwat hit me and Riyad encouraged him: 'Carry on Safwat! What do you mean by being a saint you B.......? Do you want that 30 years after your death, people will build a mausoleum in a mosque and say Zainab al-Ghazali al-Jubaili showed *karamats*[3] while imprisoned? But you're here with us and not even the devil will know what we do to you!'

I laughed in his face despite my extreme suffering. It was a mocking laugh, deriding his ignorance and arrogance: 'If we were after what you said, Allah would not have driven your evil away from us, nor would we have been able to resist and be patient and defeat what you described as Nasir's Hell. We are seekers of truth, we seek Allah and then His pleasure. Allah will see that we win over you *insha' Allah* and will grind the teeth of those you prepare to devour our flesh.'

At this, Riyad called to Safwat: 'Safwat! Help, the B...... is preaching! Safwat, she's preaching!'

Safwat rushed at me loosing his whip: 'Leave her to me Sir, and you'll see tomorrow what will happen to her.'

I was made to sit back in the water and the cell was locked.

Only Allah knows the pain and exhaustion I was suffering. An agonizing ache contorted my whole body.

'Oh poor country of mine! Have you fallen into the hands of this junta which violates all values and destroys all laws?' My thoughts distracted me from some of the pain, but added to my anxiety. What has happened, and is still happening, to me is certainly happening to others. I began imagining that the whole country had become a military prison ruled by Hamzah al-Basyuni, Safwat, Riyad the butcher and the wicked Shams Badran. They are all part of the continuous cycle which has bound this country in chains! Writers, thinkers, ministers, military leaders, ordinary citizens, the young, the elderly, men, women, the strong and the healthy, all were equal in front of their whips, their dogs, their instruments of torture. Everyone was equal, for this was the Socialism of torture!

'Poor country of mine! No, no, you won't be poor, Oh, my country, as long as you have holders of Allah's Book and inheritors of His Messenger's *Sunnah* and whoever is shaded by the umbrella of "there is no god but Allah and Muhammad is His Messenger". When we are gone, others will come after us, and after them, people who will raise the banner, and tomorrow, the Earth will shine with its Lord's light and humanity will enjoy protection by servitude to Allah, the One, the Almighty.'

From Water to the Prosecuting Attorney

Early the next morning, they took me out of the cell of water.

'You're going to the Prosecuting Attorney. Enough torture! Save yourself!' said Safwat.

'My clothes are torn; give me something to cover myself with.'

'I'll bring you a dress, and then you can write that Hasan al-Hudaibi and Sayyid Qutb agreed to kill Nasir and take over power.'

'No! No! No!'

'Then you can go naked and let your Islam prosper. Let the *Ikhwan* see you like this!'

'Allah is the One who forbears with faults, the Protector.'

I was taken to another building in the prison, and from there to a large room where a man sat behind a desk. (I was to know him later as Jalal al-Dib.) He looked at me fleetingly, giving the impression that he was smaller than the task he had been assigned to fulfil. By a gesture of his hand he signalled me to sit on a chair near his desk.

'So you're Zainab al-Ghazali, the well-known Islamic leader! Why have you put yourself through all this? Do you like what you're going through? I'm also a Muslim and one who wishes you well. I'm here to save you. I'm As'ad Fakhruddin, Prosecuting Attorney. I can't believe that the person sitting in front of me in this state is Zainab al-Ghazali. Please help me to save you from the mess you're in.'

'By Allah! We don't say except that which pleases Him and we seek none but Him.'

He frowned, looked down and asked my age.

'I was born 2nd January 1917.'

'You look over 90! Why have you done all this to yourself?'

'Nothing will happen to us except what Allah has decreed for us: He is our Lord and in Allah let the believers put their trust.'[4]

'It seems that you can't speak today!'

I did not respond.

'Over what did you agree, you and Shaykh 'Abd al-Fattah Isma'il?'

'We agreed to educate the youth on Islam, to help them understand the principles of the Book and the *Sunnah*, so that we can save this society from the loss it is suffering from.'

'I don't want preaching, I want you to clarify. Hudaibi asked you to communicate something to 'Abd al-Fattah Isma'il and something else to Sayyid Qutb. What did he communicate to you? I think the matter is clear!'

'I asked permission from the *Murshid* Hasan al-Hudaibi to bring the youth together to study the *tafsir* of the Qur'an with the help of some books of *fiqh*. Such as Ibn Hazm's *Muhalla*, books on *Tawhid* by Ibn 'Abd al-Wahhab and Ibn Taymiyyah as well as Sayyid Qutb's books. Among these youth was 'Abd al-Fattah Isma'il.'

'No Madam Zainab, this is not what happened! The whole matter is clear now so tell us the truth and save yourself.'

'All that we want is the education of a righteous generation and the building up of an Islamic *Ummah*.'

'The others have confessed to everything and laid all the blame on your shoulders.'

'Allah, Who is watching, will protect me and protect them, *insha' Allah*, from slipping into falsehood.'

'It seems that you are arrogant and very fond of showing your oratory skills. Even the prosecution cannot reach a decision about you.'

'Had the prosecution known its duties . . .'

He interrupted me furiously: 'Shut up! How dare you display your arrogance towards the prosecution!'

He called to Safwat who was by the door: 'There's no hope for her. She dares to speak badly of the prosecution. I shall write this in my minutes.'

Safwat grabbed me savagely: 'Where do you want me to take her?'

'To the water cell of course!'

I was escorted back to the water cell by Safwat who

never tired of hitting me. Satan had Safwat in his clutches, his *Jahiliyyah* had prepared him for his despotism. His twisted ego pushing him towards his superiors' pleasures, trying to draw himself nearer to them (. . . *Thus We have made alluring to each people its own doings* . . .).[5]

The Price of Meagre Sustenance!

At '*Asr* the following day, Safwat took me out of the water cell and handed me over to two more barbarians whom he commanded to take me to Cell 3. Once there, I dropped to the floor in a heap. By now my body was swollen like an inflated balloon, and I could feel my heart beating so rapidly it almost jumped from out of its place. So weak, I was unable even to groan, I submitted myself to the One Who holds in His Hands the decrees of everything.

I do not know how much time had passed when, still lying on the floor, I heard a commotion outside the cell. With extreme difficulty, I crawled to the door, and, looking through the hole in it, I could see a group of Muslim brothers standing in a long queue, each with a metal bowl in his hand. A soldier was ladling a strange substance from a large container into the bowls. When each brother had been given his share, he moved across to where two opposing rows of soldiers were standing. After finishing their meagre sustenance, the brothers were forced to walk past each soldier who flogged them as they passed by. A compulsory beating from every soldier represented payment for the most basic of foods.

One of the soldiers saw me peeping through the hole in my cell door and rushed into my cell like a crazy beast. He kicked me repeatedly, then used his whip for the final assault. Mercifully, I collapsed into unconsciousness.

The next thing I knew, Safwat was shaking me roughly. Another soldier was holding a bowl of black soup. The smell was unbearable. Safwat said to me: 'Drink this or you'll get ten floggings!'

Then, Safwat turned to the soldier and said: 'Leave her for ten minutes. If she hasn't drunk it by then, flog her and call me!'

When they left and I was sure nobody was watching, I threw the soup under the blanket they had thrown me shortly before. When the soldier returned, he found the bowl empty, took it and left.

I spent that night suffering the most excruciating pains. My body and mind a whirlpool of torment.

To Hospital

The following morning, Safwat brought Doctor Majid to my cell.

Dressed in military uniform, the doctor was accompanied by Nurse 'Abd al-Ma'bud. My feet were bleeding, my sores oozed with pus. The doctor asked the nurse to clean up my wounds as best he could. I was then taken to hospital.

In the Company of Shams!

My stay in hospital, the *Shafakhana* as they called it, was for only one day. I was happy, not only because I was far from torture, for the effects of their brutality still tormented me, but because I was grateful to see a different place. True, I was in a cell even inside the hospital, but knowing that I was away from my prison cell brought some rest to my heart. I thanked Allah for this.

The next day, back in my prison cell again, I allowed myself to dream that my stay in hospital could have been prolonged until my wounds had heeled and the pain diminished. But, soon reality came crashing back as once again I was taken to Shams Badran's office. I walked there with great difficulty because of the wounds to my feet. Indeed, I could not even walk unaided, and fell half way along that arduous journey. The soldiers dragged me the rest of the way.

No sooner did the *Jahili* butcher see me than he called for Safwat al-Rubi, his face red, his eyes stony. He turned to Safwat and pointed at me with his outstretched arm: 'Safwat, hang her in the air and give her 500 floggings.'

Such savagery cannot be outstripped, and only Shams Badran can appreciate this level of cruelty.

They suspended me on their contraption while Safwat rolled up his sleeves. Then he began to execute his orders.

'O Allah! O Allah!', I screamed.

'Where is Allah? Where is this Allah that you call? Had you asked for help from Nasir, he would have given it you immediately!', he said scornfully.

He railed against Allah, the Exalted, using the most foul and despicable language. I closed my ears to it for it was so shameful a believer would refrain from repeating it even if only to report what had been said.

The flogging over, I was brought down from that machine and made to stand. With my feet bleeding profusely, Shams Badran then ordered me to 'march on the spot' pretending that would cure my wounds!

I fell against the wall, then to the floor from sheer exhaustion. I was yanked back up only to collapse in a heap again.

'She's only acting, Pasha!', Hamzah taunted.

I lost consciousness, and woke to find a doctor examining me. He administered an injection and ordered some lemon juice which they gave me to drink. Shams Badran was still at my side: 'Heh! Obstinacy won't be of any use to you. Do as we want or we'll hang you again and again and again, if necessary a hundred times. Don't ever think that we're unable to extract what we want from you. We're just giving you a chance, do you understand? For who can stop us from burying you alive?'

'Allah will do what He wills and chooses, and to Him is praise until He is pleased!'

'Don't speak in that language and style to me, B.........!' Safwat then handed me a pen and paper: 'You know what is required, no need for philosophy! Write down everything you know, O you *Ikhwan* liars!, and how you were going to kill Nasir. Understood! Go on B.........!'

He locked the door and left.

I could not hold the pen, for my hands were too swollen. The day passed without me writing a single word. Safwat came back to collect the papers but when he saw I had written nothing he shouted that he would leave the papers a little longer for me to save myself!

I began writing with extreme difficulty, and on the third day Hamzah al-Basyuni came and took the papers. I spent the rest of the day between sleep and waking, for I could not settle in one position: if I stood up, I experienced terrible pain from my sore and bleeding feet, and if I lay down my swollen body tormented me.

The following day I was dragged again to Shams Badran's office. Tearing up my papers, he screamed: 'You B........! Isn't all the torture you went through enough! What is this that you've written? Nonsense! Hamzah, flog her!'

'It's better we take her back to the dogs', intervened Khalil and al-Basyuni.

'Bring the dogs here, Safwat!'

Safwat rushed out, returning with two huge dogs, obviously from among the ones I had encountered in the early days of my imprisonment in 'Egypt's Bastille.'[6] Within seconds they were upon me, my only consolation being the following which I repeated continuously: 'Allah is Sufficient unto us, and He is the best Disposer of affairs! O Allah! Relieve me from evil with whatever You want and in whatever manner You want.'

'B.........! Write that you conspired to kill Nasir! And how you were to kill him. Write! Write you B........!', cursed Shams Badran.

The number of dogs became three: two devouring my flesh, the other, Shams Badran, cursing me with his impudent tongue! Eventually, realizing the futility of all this he called off the dogs, demanding instead that I be flogged. But this too was averted by calls for a doctor to examine me.

The doctor advised against further flogging, my being too weak to sustain it. I was taken to Cell 24, a cell to which I had not been before. There I was made to stand and await my deliverance. In the middle of the cell was a fire, and at each corner a soldier, each of them proudly displaying their snake-like whips. One of them hit me so that I was forced towards the fire, but when I tried to turn away from the flames another hit me to turn me back again and so on and so forth. All the while the heat of the fire scorched my exposed flesh. I was tortured in this way for about two hours, between the flames of the fire which I was scared of falling into and the searing lashes of their whips.

Hamzah al-Basyuni came in, repeating his deluded nonsense: either I confirm the plot to assassinate Nasir, or else. In any case I lost consciousness and when I awoke I was once again in hospital.

Games for the Media

One morning, the soldiers came and took me out of the hospital cell into the courtyard where a number of cameramen had gathered. I was made to sit, then told to cross my legs and put a cigarette in my mouth so that they could take photographs of me.

'It is out of the question for me to take hold of a cigarette or put it in my mouth.'

Determined to get the photographs, they put the barrel of a gun into my mouth and another to my temple. But still I refused and pronounced the *shahadah*.

'Do as you will, I am not doing it!', I told them.

For my refusal to submit, I was flogged, and again a gun was put to my head with the demand that I take the cigarette in my mouth. But I persisted in my refusal. Finally, in despair, they took photographs of me without crossed legs and without a cigarette.

The following day, they asked me to relay on television something they had written for me about the *Ikhwan*.

'If I appear on television I will not say other than this: "Nasir is a *kafir* who is fighting Islam by persecuting the *Ikhwan* group. This is why we are resisting him. He says that rule by the Qur'an is backwardness, decadence and repugnant fanaticism. Yet, he imports his laws and legislation from the Soviet Union with its ungodly, atheistic system. This is why we are fighting him and will continue to do so".'

'We'll make you say what we want, how we want; we'll use all the force that it takes.'

'Yesterday I refused to put a cigarette in my mouth despite the fact that I had a gun pointed at my head. Do you think that I will say other than the truth? No, by Allah! We are the holders of a message and the trustees of an *ummah*. Inheritors of a Book!'

With that I was repeatedly flogged and then taken back to my cell.

Room 32

I was supposed to have been arrested for a specific crime. If this was so, why did they persist in trying to get

me to say that I conspired to kill Nasir, that I planned
this crime? If all the details of this crime were available,
as they said, why this persistent demand to confess the
crime? Why ask me to give proof of a crime which existed
only in their imaginations? The reason was clear: all their
torturous efforts were directed at one goal - at fighting
Islam and destroying its foundations.

'Are you still alive you B..........?', shouted Shams Badran
as I was again dragged into his office. 'I told you Hamzah
to bring me her dead body!'

'Sorry Pasha! Tell her your instructions and she's ready
to execute them.'

'Write you B..........!'

'I won't write anything except the truth. If you want to
kill me, then do so. For it is a martyrdom that will be
written with Allah, the Exalted.'

'We won't allow you this martyrdom!', snarled Hasan
Khalil.

'Martyrdom is with Allah. If He wants it for anyone of
His servants, He will give it.'

Recognizing my persistence, Shams's anger was
overwhelming: 'Hang her in the air and flog her 500
times, so that she can know her God!'

The flogging over, and God alone knows how I bore it,
I was then forced to listen to Shams Badran's pathetic
remonstrations: 'Sit here! Do you think that our hearts
are made of stone. I'm deeply affected by your state, my
father after all is a shaykh in al-Azhar University!'

I looked at him with the utmost disdain. That he could
not swallow, and quickly reverted to his bestiality: 'You
B........! Hamzah, take her to 32!'

I was pushed into a cell in which there were two
wooden posts connected to each other at the top by a
horizontal post. From these, two spheres were suspended.
I was made to stand on a chair, and encouraged by their
whips ordered to take hold of the two spheres. Then, as

quick as a flash, they pulled the chair from underneath my feet, leaving me dangling in the air!

Unable to stay suspended in that manner for more than a few minutes, I fell to the floor. The butchers pounced on me with their whips and forced me back up. Again I fell, only to be repeatedly flogged. This pattern continued for nearly three hours, my tortured body covered in congealing blood.

Betrayal Replaced by Loftiness

When they took me back to Shams Badran's office, he repeated his noxious command to write what they prescribed.

'I won't write anything that is not true.'

'We know everything, anyway. The *Ikhwan* have confessed it all. Read the files for her!' 'Abd al-Fattah Isma'il's file, Majid 'Abd al-'Aziz and Ahmad 'Abd al-Majid's files, Muhammad Qutb's, Yusuf Hawash's, Sabri 'Arafah's, 'Abd al-Majid al-Shadhili's, Faruq al-Manshawi's, and Mursi Mustafa Mursi's files. Read them all to her.'

Jalal al-Dib began reading 'Ali al-'Ashmawi's statement and I was truly shocked. When he had finished, Shams closed one of his eyes, shook his head, and said: 'What do you think of that then?'

'It's all lies and slander!'

'Do you deny that you established the *Ikhwan* Organization? Your leader's statement shows that you founded the Organization. Jalal, read al-Hudaibi's statement to her.'

Then he asked him to leave that file for a while and read 'Abd al-Fattah Isma'il's statement, and when Jalal had finished reading, Shams turned to me: 'What do you think?'

I did not answer.

'Read for her what the architect of the *Ikhwan*, Sayyid Qutb, has said!', Shams instructed Jalal.

Jalal began reading, first from one file then another, and when he had finished Shams Badran again asked: 'What do you think about all you've heard now? Are you going to write what we want?'

'All this is false!'

'And what is right, you prodigy of your time?'

'I believe that everything that is written here as being from 'Ali al-'Ashmawi is false. As for the other brothers, they are people of *da'wah* and truth and what is attributed to them is nothing but a forgery.'

'Safwat! Hang her in the air! And bring 'Ali al-'Ashmawi and the dogs!'

When 'Ashmawi came in he was wearing clean, elegant pyjamas made of fine silk. His hair was combed and he bore no signs of physical torture. As I looked at him and contemplated my own state and that of my brothers, I was convinced that he had betrayed Allah's trust. Had confessed to false and slanderous things. He had slipped into the abyss of these perverts, had become one of Shams Badran's men. He had joined the ranks of those who know no virtue, manners or *din*.

''Ali! What did you take from Zainab al-Ghazali last time you went to see her and what did she tell you?', Shams enquired of him.

'She gave me E£1000, and told me that other monies were with Ghadah 'Amar which were to be kept at al-Hudaibi's house or Qutb's. If she were arrested I was to contact Ghadah or Hamidah who would know where the money was if we needed it.'

'Zainab! How much money was this and why were you so concerned about it?'

'The money totalled around E£4000, and represented the membership fees of a group of the *Ikhwan* from Sudan and Saudi Arabia. It was to help the families of those imprisoned as well as contribute to the expenses of school and university students and their rents. We spent E£1000 of it on these families and the person standing in front of you, 'Ali 'Ashmawi, took that E£1000 to give to 'Abd al-Fattah Isma'il for this purpose.'

'Ali! What did you eat at Zainab's house the last time you went to see her?'

'She gave me rice with liver and told me: "Eat! May Allah help you!" '

'That's enough! Go now 'Ali.'

'Ali left, safe in the care that Shams Badran had enticed him with.

Shortly after, Hamzah al-Basyuni came back with 'Abd al-Fattah Isma'il. The latter's countenance bore a truthful gravity and shone with the light of the believers. His blue prison uniform was torn and signs of physical torture bespoke what this truthful, believing *mujahid* had endured.

'*Assalam 'alaykum!*', he addressed me.

'*Wa 'alaykum assalam wa rahmat Allah!*'

'Abd al-Fattah, what were you doing at Zainab's house and why did you repeatedly visit her house?', teased Shams.

'She is my sister in Allah. We were helping each other to educate the Muslim youth on the principles of the Qur'an and the *Sunnah*. Of course, this would eventually lead to a change in the nature of the State: from a State of *Jahiliyyah* to an Islamic State.'

'Stop your preaching. You're not on a pulpit you B............! Get out! Get out!'

And 'Abd al-Fattah left, after wishing me well.

The steadfast manhood displayed by 'Abd al-Fattah gave me a sense of peace. For it emanated from the *iman* in Allah that is in him. I said secretly to myself: 'Praise be to Allah, Allah has real men. May You protect them for Your own *da'wah*. If 'Ashmawi has betrayed us, there are still patient, believing people: leaders of the way and seekers of the truth.'

'Take the B........! I want her back here tomorrow with the required written papers!', bellowed Shams.

Hasan Khalil handed a pen and paper to Safwat and I was taken back to hospital. I took the pen, but what was I to write? Did they want me to anger my Lord and oppose our religion? No, by Allah! I will not write anything except that I have acted in the way of Allah and under the banner of Allah. I believe in Him only and I do not worship any except Him. O Lord! Pour constancy on us and make our steps firm and take our souls as Muslims. As for you Pharaohs of your time, you only seek the life of this world, soon you will know what vicissitudes your affairs will take with Allah.

Continuous Onslaught

To spare you, dear reader, who has already suffered much of my endurance with me, from too much more heartfelt anguish, I will not continue to document each and every bout of the barbarism I suffered. Suffice to say I was repeatedly, over a period of several weeks, taken from hospital to Shams Badran's office and back again. If I was too weak to walk or be dragged, then I was taken on a stretcher. Their whips continued to lacerate wounds already seriously infected. Wounds only barely treated to enable further flayings. When I could stand no more and collapsed from exhaustion, I would be thrashed still more while suspended from one contraption or another. Even my unconscious state did not deter them; I was injected with the most noxious substances to bring me round again, to endure yet more torture. More suffering, more inhumanity, more ignominy. My tormentors' whips would be interchanged for dogs, and dogs for enforced, unbearable standing, hour after hour, night after night, often in front of huge air-conditioning machines, their noise and heat an agonizing torrid wave of infliction.

Near death on so many occasions, my salvation was with Allah. Through His guidance alone I was able to endure. And all the time my oppressors, Hell-bent on their illusions, their altars an insatiable quest for power, persisted in untruths. Beside themselves at my resistance, they would tear at their hair, slap their own faces, beat and pound their chests, gesticulate madly. To no avail. For Allah is with those who believe, with those who follow His path.

Extracts

'. . . Since neither the dogs, water, fire, whips nor any of this torture has worked on you, the Pasha will slaughter you today. For he has his orders from Nasir to do so.'

'The One who does is Allah!'

'You want us to do like you, and fail as you've failed! You want us to leave the Soviet Union who rules half the world and yield to the words of somebody like al-Hudaibi, Sayyid Qutb or Hasan al-Banna! You're crazy! We're not like you! Answer me!'

'(For they, when they were told that there is no God except Allah, would puff themselves up with pride. And say: "What! Shall we give up our gods for the sake of a Poet possessed?".⁷ These gods were idols, and the rulers are the custodians of idols. It was they who accused the Prophet (peace be upon him) of insanity. And, thus, is history repeating itself. You say to those who call you to Allah, you are insane. The despot directs you to commit falsehood. You follow him, humiliated, for cheap rewards. You please a creature to anger the Creator!'

'You want us to revert back to stagnation and backwardness? By Allah, Zainab! I fear, and feel pity, for you.'

'(. . . For us Allah suffices and He is the best Disposer of affairs).' Fear and pity! What is this? The case as you say has come to light, so what do you care about my confession and avowal? The only thing that is clear is your lies, falsehoods, and incriminations of innocent people.

――――――●―――――――

'. . . Forget your obstinacy. I want you to write what we want!'

'Do you want me to write that we conspired to kill Nasir? This is out of the question. By Allah! We met for nothing other than study of the Qur'an and *Hadith*, to explain to people how to rid themselves of the worship of despots and worship Allah instead, so that they can adore Him alone and establish His religion. We called people to obey the commandments of the Qur'an and the *Sunnah* and not to deviate from Islam's teachings. The present regime is a *Jahili* regime, one which should be abolished not by force but by the existence of vast Islamically dedicated grassroots from the *Ummah*. Therefore, why do you accuse us of conspiring to kill Nasir? We first have to get you out of *Jahiliyyah*, and when the vast dedicated grassroots are formed, an Islamic state will be established for sure. No! No! I won't write what you want! I won't! Kill me, for my life is nothing for me!'

――――――●―――――――

'. . . In the papers you've written so far, which I tore up, you didn't mention anything about 'Abd al-'Aziz 'Ali.'

'Who is 'Abd al-'Aziz 'Ali?'

''Abd al-'Aziz 'Ali Pasha whom Nasir promoted to a Minister but who was ungrateful and bit the hand that fed him, turning against Nasir.'

''Abd al-'Aziz 'Ali, the man of the "Black Hand"

movement against the British, is one of the great men of the Nationalist Party. Nasir and his colleagues sat at his feet to learn lessons of patriotism from him. I know he's a great man, a friend of my husband's, a brother in Allah and his wife besides being a friend and a sister to me, is also a member of the Muslim Ladies Group.'

'Did you make him join the *Ikhwan*?'

'It would have been an honour for he is, like al-Khansa'[8] said: ". . . A banner lit on top by fire".'

'. . . We want to know why you introduced 'Abd al-'Aziz to 'Abd al-Fattah Isma'il, and where such an introduction took place?'

'It happened when I broke my leg because of your secret agents' treachery. He visited me in hospital with his wife, and visits to my house continued when I left hospital. It just so happened that one day 'Abd al-Fattah Isma'il came to visit me and 'Abd al-'Aziz was already there, so they were introduced. This is all that I remember about it.'

'Madam Zainab! We'll assume this time that this introduction took place by sheer coincidence, but tell us, how was 'Abd al-'Aziz 'Ali introduced, in your home, to Farid 'Abd al-Khaliq?'

'When the nurse came to my house to provide my rehabilitation treatment, 'Abd al-'Aziz left my personal room and sat in the living room. Meanwhile, Farid 'Abd al-Khaliq also arrived and waited in the living room for me. At that time they did not know each other. When my treatment was over, I introduced them.'

'. . . Are you still alive? After all that's happened to you, you're still alive?'

119

'Allah said: (. . . *Woe to the makers of the pit (of fire))*.[9]
Those who killed the believers in the pit of fire were
blinded by falsehood and slander. As for those who were
killed, they were people carrying a message and trust,
they were adamant in handing over that trust so as to
convey their message.'

'You crazy woman! We don't understand what you're
saying and we're not the least moved by your style of
talking. Do you still believe in the existence of a god?
You have been defeated since 1948: you were defeated
when you resisted Faruq, you were defeated when you
resisted the revolution in 1954 and you were defeated
when you resisted the revolution in 1965. So where is
your alleged God?'

'We won in 1948, we won in 1954 and we won in 1965!'

'We hang you in the air like a chicken, we throw you
in water like a fish, into fire like a dried stick and we
even loose our dogs on you. If your God really exists,
you defeated B........!, why did He not stop us from doing
all this to you?'

'It's an illusion that you've defeated us with all this
flogging and torture. The truth of the matter is that
you're scared of us!'

'Shut up! You're nothing but criminals!'

'Nay! We are not criminals! We are holders of a message
and trustees of a nation. Callers of truth and signposts in
the way of light!'

'Explain to me how you have defeated us!'

'We have defeated you for as long as we are rich by
Allah, strong by Him, relying on Him, struggling and
fighting for His sake. Only one thing will prove that we
are defeated, and that is if we abandon our belief in the
necessity of *Jihad* to establish *Tawhid* and elevate the
word of Islam. Islam in its essence is a religion and state,
a policy for internal and foreign affairs, a system for the
Ummah and society. Islam is a peace which will fill the

world with justice and liberate people from idol worship and replace it with worship of Allah, the Mighty. The servant who submits his face to Allah in truth and sincerity becomes linked to Him, the Exalted, the Lord of Everything, so why would this servant fear other creatures when his spirit is related to heaven and its gardens. As for you, misguided disbelievers, what do you have at your disposal? You tear our bodies, you kill us, you terrorize us, you deny us food and water. The whips are in your hand, the means of torture are under your command, but for us all this is futile. Why are you scared of us? Because we are the party of Allah and you are the party of Satan (*"Those who resist Allah and His Apostle will be among those most humiliated. Allah has decreed 'It is I and My apostles who must prevail': for Allah is one full of strength, able to enforce His Will"*).'[10]

'Safwat! Suspend her in the air and flog her!'

'. . . B..........! Obstinacy won't be of any use to you. Give up your obstinacy so that we can finish our investigations and send you to the prosecution.'

'Prosecution! And who are you then?'

'We are preparing you for the prosecution!'

'What do you want from me?'

'Be steady in your answer, for you don't have any strength left for resistance, and as you know Safwat is always ready!'

'Allah is the Doer, the Helper!'

'Why did Muhammad Qutb and the *Ikhwan*'s youth gather in your house?'

'Professor Muhammad Qutb and his sisters Aminah and Hamidah regularly visited me at home . . .'

'Muhammad Qutb and the *Ikhwan*'s youth, you B........!, met at your house, why?'

'Our righteous, active youth would sometimes visit me at the same time as did Muhammad Qutb, by sheer coincidence . . .'

'You B.........! I know the youth asked you to arrange meetings with Muhammad Qutb. Why?'

'When Professor Muhammad Qutb published his two books, *The Pagan Ignorance of the 20th Century* [Jahilyyat al-Qarn al-'Ishrin] and *Evolution and Permanence* [al-Tatawwur wa al-Thabat] some of my children and brothers from *da'wah* asked me to arrange a meeting in order to ask a number of questions relating to these books which were not clear to them, and the Professor obliged.'

'Why did 'Abd al-Fattah Isma'il attend these meetings?'

'Because he is one of the best among the *Ikhwan*'s youth and among its chosen men.'

'Indeed, what good folk, B......! At which of these meetings did Muhammad Qutb agree with 'Abd al-Fattah Isma'il to kill Nasir?'

'The story of assassinating Nasir is one of your invention!'

'B.....! Your end will be in my hands today.'

'. . . B........! You don't have the strength left to endure our tortures, so have pity on yourself or I swear by the head of Nasir that I will bury you with al-Fayyumi and the others!'

'Listen Zainab! Listen to what the Pasha is saying and think of yourself. Let us reach a solution with you!'

'A man came to you on behalf of Fu'ad Siraj al-Din and asked you to reach an agreement with the *Ikhwan* to collaborate with the Wafd Party to remove Nasir from power. This man told you that there are men in Field Marshal 'Amir's office who can co-operate with you and the Wafd Party.'

'This is an utter lie! Fu'ad Siraj al-Din did not send anybody to me about this issue or any other issue. In fact I have not seen Fu'ad Pasha for the last 12 years. To be more precise, I would say that my husband, al-Haj Muhammad Salim Salim, was at an auction where he met, by chance, his Eminence Fu'ad Siraj al-Din who asked about my health and asked my husband to convey to me his regards and best wishes.'

'Did Fu'ad Siraj al-Din send for you or not?'

'He did not!'

———————————•———————————

'. . . There is no god but Allah, the Doer, and Allah is Sufficient unto us and He is the best Disposer of affairs. O Lord! Pour on us patience and make us die as Muslims!'

'Safwat! Bring the dogs!'

'O Allah! I seek refuge in Your pleasure from Your anger! O Allah! Drive away evil from me with whatever You want and in whatever way You want it.'

———————————•———————————

'. . . Woman be reasonable! We feel for you, for we're not monsters like you say! And Nasir has a big heart. He will forgive you if you speak the truth. Act for your own benefit. Zainab! Tell the truth!'

'The truth! Tell Nasir he is the usurper who violated Allah's authority. Repent to Allah and come back to Him. Leave your falsehood, injustice and darkness and come back to truth, justice and light. Those who are supporting you in your injustice and whom you are using as tools for your crime, falsehood and aggression are sick in the heart and you are sick too!'

'Is this the message you want us to convey to Nasir?'

'I have said it, so report it to him.'

'Where are the dogs that you have kept hungry since yesterday Hamzah? Where are they?'

'Zainab, you can't do this to yourself, you're near death. Save yourself! None of the *Ikhwan* is going to help you; they have all acted for their own benefit. I have begged the Pasha to bring 'Ali 'Ashmawi to remind you of the person who came to see you on behalf of Fu'ad Siraj al-Din.'

'B.......! Remember or we'll confront you with 'Ali 'Ashmawi!'

''Ali 'Ashmawi has sold himself to despots of crime and falsehood at a cheap price. For that he has lost this world and the World-to-Come. As for the story of Siraj al-Din, it is pure fabrication.'

'Zainab! I will remind you of something that may help your memory of Siraj al-Din. You know al-Husaini 'Abd al-Ghaffar, he was with the *Ikhwan*, then left to join "the Youth of Sayyidina Muhammad" (Shabab Sayyidina Muhammad).[11] You spoke with him several times trying to persuade him to return to the *Ikhwan*.'

'Allah is Sufficient unto us and He is the best Disposer of affairs! Al-Husaini 'Abd al-Ghaffar is my brother in Allah; he was so when he was with the *Ikhwan* and remained so with "the Youth of Sayyidina Muhammad". Indeed, I asked him to come back to the *Ikhwan* but he refused. He has nothing to do with Siraj al-Din or the Wafd. At that time he was President of The Free Constitutionalist's Youth (Shabab al-Ahrar al-Dusturiyyin) and that makes him an opponent of al-Wafd not an ally.'

'This is true but when it is a question of getting an agreement with the Constitutionalists, the Sa'dists,[12] the Wafdists and the *Ikhwan*, then it is all too natural.'

'This is not true; there is a gap between the *Ikhwan* and those who have not studied Islam and its way of life which is based upon Divine Guidance.'

'Please Pasha, let her finish. Carry on Zainab!'

'As for the *Ikhwan*, they take Islam as an *'Aqidah*, search its origins and scrutinize its sources as received from Allah through the Prophet (peace be upon him) and through the Book and the *Sunnah*. The *Ikhwan* have a special love for this country. For as long as it is the land of Islam, they will defend its borders and for its sake they will be martyred. They liberate the land for Allah as they liberate the people for Allah, they return the land to Allah as they return people to Allah. And in the land that worships Allah and with the people who worship Him will the *Ummah* and Muslim Society be established. Muhammad (peace be upon him) did not liberate, at the beginning of his mission, the land then call for *Tawhid*, nor did he call for social reform and then invite people to *Tawhid*, nor did he call for an equitable repartition of wealth then for *Tawhid*: he did not call for partial reform but called people to *Tawhid*. Muhammad (peace be upon him) called for *Tawhid* and so many people accepted Islam. They believed with him that there is none to be worshipped except Allah, to none is sovereignty due except Allah, none provides livelihood except Allah, none can do real harm or good except Allah. It is He Who takes life away and He Who gives life, there is no disposer or legislator except He. When these meanings had sunk deep into Muslims' minds, the *hijrah* to Madinah took place by the very first few who accepted Islam. Then, there was the first call to establish the *Ummah*. After that, the Qur'an continued to be revealed to the Prophet (peace be upon him) bringing legislation and punishment, *halal* and *haram*. The *Ummah* was truly established and the earth was filled with justice, light and truth.'

'After all this pathetic nonsense are you going to relate Siraj al-Din's story?'

'This story is something you fabricated. Those who reported it are telling lies. I do not have anything to tell about Siraj al-Din except that he was a patriotic man who

served his country, and that I think he is now retired.'
'Safwat, bring the dogs!'

---------•---------

('. . . *O fire! Be you cool, and (a means of) safety for
Abraham!*')[13] May You be blessed and exalted, O Lord!
For I am the grandchild of Abraham, the first monotheist
and the Prophet's grandfather. Have mercy on me for
what I am enduring from the devils who are not pleased
with me, because of my saying: 'my Lord is Allah and I
associate with Him none!' (*Say: O you that reject Faith! I
worship not that which you worship . . .*)[14]

---------•---------

'. . . Tell us Zainab! What was al-Husaini 'Abd al-
Ghaffar's opinion about what reached you from Fu'ad
Siraj al-Din? And who were the people that were going
to help Fu'ad Siraj al-Din from Field Marshal 'Amir's
office? And what did he ask from the *Ikhwan* in order to
carry out the *coup*?'
'Al-Husaini 'Abd al-Ghaffar is my brother in Allah and
I do not know anything about these lies and falsehood!'
'Listen Zainab! Didn't al-Husaini meet 'Abd al-Fattah
Isma'il in your house? Did you not ask al-Husaini to join
the ranks of the *Ikhwan*?'
'I spoke with al-Husaini about joining the ranks of
da'wah; this is not a crime. Al-Husaini is a man who
believes in the *Ikhwan's da'wah* even though he is not one
of its members: he wishes that its aims are achieved and
that people are guided by the Book and its goals, the
Sunnah and its aims. Al-Husaini met 'Abd al-Fattah
Isma'il in my house and spoke about Islam and the
decadence that had befallen Muslims, and then he left.
This meeting took place by coincidence. When he left,

'Abd al-Fattah Isma'il told me that al-Husaini was a righteous, good man and a sincere scholar with a strong sufi background.'

'Al-Husaini has confessed everything. We'll give you one last chance to rethink your position *vis-à-vis* the Wafdists and the men working in Field Marshal 'Amir's office. We'll even confront you with al-Husaini and Fu'ad Siraj al-Din but only after we've pulled your eyes out!'

'Praise be to Allah (. . . *Truly it is not their eyes that are blind, but their hearts which are in their breasts).'*[15]

'Safwat, bring the dogs!'

'The end is in the hands of Allah not in your hands, Allah is the Doer, the Mighty, the Firm!'

———————————— • ————————————

. . . al-Husaini 'Abd al-Ghaffar was brought in. His arm was in plaster and his feet a mass of bandages. The signs of monstrous torture were apparent all over his body. We greeted each other.

'What is your story about Zainab, al-Husaini?'

'It's all written and the papers are with you!'

These papers were given to al-Husaini to read. I was convinced that he had been tortured until he had admitted all they wanted, for he related many things which I felt he never believed in, spoke about or called for. All that he read was untrue, just sick imaginings. I was asked for my opinion.

'It's nothing but torture and persecution to force the *Ikhwan* to say what you want.'

'Is what you heard a lie?'

'Al-Husaini does not lie, but I am sure that he was tortured until . . .'

'What do you mean? Didn't he say the things that he just read to you? Do you want to burn yourself for the sake of al-Husaini as you burned for the *Ikhwan*?'

I turned to al-Husaini and asked him: 'Did you convey a message from Pasha Fu'ad Siraj al-Din?'

'Little Siraj al-Din not his Eminence the Pasha!'

'I don't know anyone except Pasha Siraj al-Din. Who is Little Fu'ad?'

'Pasha Fu'ad's cousin.'

'And what about him?'

'I told them it was a joke that Sulaiman 'Ali told me and which I related in front of you *Hajjah* Zainab!'

'Allah is Sufficient unto us and He is the best Disposer of affairs! You oppressors have made out of a joke a conspiracy and even Fu'ad Pasha is not spared by you!', I recalled.

'. . . I have dictated to 'Abd al-Ma'bud nothing except that which pleases Allah, He is our Lord and the best Helper!'

'You B.........! Do you want to destroy all the previous investigations and annul all the *Ikhwan*'s confessions? What the *Ikhwan* said is right! You are bound to approve what they said, you are bound by everything they said!'

'I am only bound by the truth that I believe in, I am not bound to say anything except that which I believe in, nor am I bound to believe that these are my brothers' answers. Confront me with all of them! It is your torture and whips that have extracted these answers from them!'

'Hamzah take her! I want her dead body and I'll sign the permission to bury her!'

'. . . Zainab! If you co-operate with us, you'll meet with Nasir tomorrow, and you can go home right now. The ban on your Group will be reversed and a sum of E£50,000 will be given as help to your Group, by way of a first instalment for building on the land that belongs to the Group in Misr al-Jadidah. Plus there'll be an extra E£10,000 to re-issue your magazine!'

'Zainab! Has the Muslim Ladies Group land in Misr al-Jadidah?', another man called Salah Nasr, asked.

'Yes! It has 60,000 square metres.'

'What was the Group going to do with this large area of land?'

'The Muslim Ladies Group was going to build a home for educating Muslim girls, a guest house for Muslim ladies, a lecture hall, and headquarters for the Group, a Mosque, a primary and intermediary school and a college for female preachers.'

'Where was the money to do all this coming from?'

'From donations and continual hard work.'

'Then, President Nasir's offer represents a significant opportunity for you. You go back home, and the Group is revitalized! The President's trust has great results!'

'Our trust in Allah is greater! Allah is greater in ourselves than the earth, money and all the despots of the earth who have violated Allah's and the people's rights. I don't want anything from you, and I will never agree to meet Nasir nor shake the hands that are soiled with the blood of Isma'il al-Fayyumi, Rif'at Bakr, Muhammad 'Awad, 'Abd al-Qadir 'Awdah and his friends and others. The blood that has been shed will lead Muslims throughout the following generations back to their glorious, bright past, to the seat of responsibility in this world.'

'Hamzah! Take her to room 34!'

————————◆————————

'. . . Zainab! Three years ago, a meeting of more than 50 *Ikhwan* members from all over the country, took place in your house. What happened at this meeting?'

'We prayed *Maghrib, 'Isha* and *tarawih* in congregation!'
'I'm asking you about the purpose of this meeting.'
'I don't remember!'
'Did they have the breaking-of-the-fast dinner at your place?'
'A number of them.'
'What was the meeting for?'
'We were studying Islam and how to counter the current of atheism that was supported and fed by the institutions of *Jahiliyyah* and its media.'
'And why specifically at your place?'
'Because I am from among the Muslims, *insha' Allah!*'
'What *Jahiliyyah*, Islam and atheism are you talking about?'
'If you travel across the country you will see on the streets, and on the footpaths scores of atheistic newspapers, magazines and cheap periodicals calling for a loosening of manners. Their aim is to propagate Communism, atheism, prolixity and a general loosening of character . . .'
'That's enough! Enough! This is nonsense! Give me the names of those who were present at that meeting!'
'I don't remember their names.'
'A man present at the meeting left to meet al-Hudaibi then came back after you contacted al-Hudaibi's home. Who is this man?'
'I don't remember! All that I remember in this respect is that he requested me to ask al-Hudaibi's consent about me meeting him, so what's wrong with that?'
'Why did you meet? I will make the question easier for you. The man who went to al-Hudaibi was 'Abd al-Fattah al-Sharif, was he not? I'll hang you in the air if you don't answer! You agreed to kill Nasir and overthrow the government.'
'We agreed to fight *Jahiliyyah*, prolixity and atheism and work towards spreading the teachings of the Qur'an.

130

We agreed to show Muslims their obligatory duty in
establishing the rule of the Qur'an and the *Sunnah*.'
'And what is al-Azhar doing? Speak up, what is the duty
of al-Azhar? Safwat, hang her in the air and flog her!'

All this was done in the name of authority, in the
name of Egypt. Nasir and his agents satisfying their
desire for vengeance, planning the destruction of the
religion of Islam. By murdering its proponents, and
spreading their banner of *kufr* and atheism. For when the
keys to authority fall into the hands of the heedless and
the ignorant, then that authority turns into domination,
opinion into a curse, power into deceit. From such whims,
all that is established is counterfeit.

Notes and References

1. A Turkish military and civil title of high rank. It is still used
in some Arab countries to designate a civil authority. Cf. *The Concise
Encyclopaedia of Islam*.

2. *Al-Baqarah*: 258.

3. (Lit. acts of generosity. Sing. *Karamah*). Gifts or powers of a
spiritual or psychic nature acquired by a saint, short of miracle
working. Cf. *The Concise Encyclopaedia of Islam*.

4. *Al-Tawbah*: 51.

5. *Al-An'am*: 108.

6. The Bastille is an old, rather infamous, prison of the French
monarchy.

7. *Al-Saffat*: 36.

8. A famous poetess of the late *Jahiliyyah* period and early Islam,
well known for the elegiac poetry she wrote, in *Jahiliyyah*, bewailing
her brother.

9. *Al-Buruj*: 4.

10. *Al-Mujadalah*: 20.

11. An Islamic group whose members were part of the *Ikhwan*, but later formed their own group following differences in methodology between them and Hasan al-Banna.

12. A party founded in 1938, following a split in the Wafd Party.

13. *Al-Anbiya'*: 69.

14. *Al-Kafirun*: 1-2.

15. *Al-Hajj*: 46.

CHAPTER 5

Facing Up to Nasir

I lay motionless on the floor, in front of them, as if dead. I could see my wounds had been treated and then from the corner of my eye I saw Nasir holding a pair of black glasses in his hand, leaning on 'Abd al-Hakim 'Amir's shoulder. I immediately forgot my pain and a strange sense of awakening crept into my body. I felt a great vitality! I was given a glass of lemon juice, then I was picked up and made to sit on a chair. I was offered coffee which I accepted without hesitation.

I had the feeling that something important was about to happen.

Shams Badran spoke: 'Zainab. You woman! I want you to answer every question I ask or else! Suppose that the *Ikhwan* are ruling the country and that we are standing in front of you for trial, what would you do to us?'

'We don't dwell in the venues of those who have committed injustices against themselves, nor do we sully our hands with what they have sullied theirs with. We don't immerse our hands in blood. We do not sit in the seats of the despots of the earth!'

'Shut up! I asked you a question: If you were sitting where I am now, what would you do with me?'

'We are seekers of truth and leaders of a way of life, we are not contemplating taking over power. We are holders of the banner of "there is no god but Allah" that we give our wealth and lives for (*Allah has purchased of the believers their persons and their goods; for theirs (in return) is Paradise . . .).*[1]

'Shut up you B.........! I repeat, what would you have done to us had you taken over power?'

'We are not seekers of power, and we are not bothered whether we are at the top of responsibility or its bottom. We are guardians of the way that leads to the man who carries the trust and is elected by the *Ummah*, as Allah's bondsman who rules by Allah's revelation, so that this abode becomes an abode of Islamic Renaissance.'

'Shut up! Shut up! Shut up! I want one single answer: Had you been sitting in the chair I am sitting in now, what would you have done with me as the accused in front of you?'

'It will, probably, take many generations before Islam rules. We don't anticipate the phases. And when Islam rules, women's position will be at its proper place whereby they can educate the men of this *Ummah*.'

'You B.........! Just suppose hypothetically that you are sitting in my place, what would you do with me?'

'Islam is justice, light and mercy. In Islam there are no whips, no killings, no torture, prisons, expulsions, burying of people alive, nor tearing bodies apart. There is no displacement of children, widowing of women, pharaohs or idol-worship. In Islam, there is nothing but truth and justice, a word is confronted with a word and an argument with an argument.'

'Safwat, suspend her in the air and flog her!'

'We want her alive so that she can stand trial.'

'Yes! Yes!', said Shams. 'We want her to live and to stand trial so that people can see her and take her as the example she is.'

'We need medicines, now, which we don't have here.'

'Get them from Field Marshal 'Amir's chemist shop.'

I was moved to hospital and I do not recollect what happened that night, for I was unconscious and remained so for three days.

It All Started as a Joke!

I heard the voices of Murad and Safwat as they left Brother Ahmad Kamal's cell. They were asking him for the address of Sayf al-Banna the son of *Shahid* Hasan al-Banna. He gave it to them. They returned a few hours later for his office address.

I began to pray for Sayf, for his mother and brothers. His mother had a serious heart condition and he was the only breadwinner in the family. I begged Allah to drive away the ugly plans these people had prepared for them. I was taken on a stretcher to Shams Badran.

'Didn't I tell you this woman would not enter my office again alive! Why have you brought her to me alive?'

'It is neither according to your will nor mine that I should live or die, it is Allah's Will, He is the Bestower of life and death!'

'Shut up B.........! Just answer me, who was supposed to assassinate Nasir on his way to Alexandria?'

Hasan Khalil intervened: 'Shall I make the question a little more accessible for her, Pasha?'

Shams nodded his head in agreement.

'A man told you about a group of people waiting for Nasir in the Sahara, as he was on his way to Alexandria. Who was this man? Who was in the jeep waiting to kill Nasir?'

'Answer quickly!', Shams added.

'How futile are the things that you torture people for! Woe to you from Allah! Woe to you from history! Woe to you from all the people who will curse you!'

My reward for this would be more broken bones. Broken ribs, broken phalanges, broken everywhere.

'If we suspend you now in the air you'll die, but we'll forgive you if you tell us the story! Tell us the story from the beginning. B........! Tell us the story that Sayf al-Banna related to you.'

'You mean the joke he told me!'

Badran lunged at me, slapped me on the face and kicked me repeatedly, saying: 'Yes, the joke!'

'I was at al-Banna's house. Sayf told me what others had related to him, that Nasir was travelling, by car, along the Saharan route to Alexandria, and that a group of military men planned to ambush him. At the last minute, the itinerary was changed and Nasir travelled by train. And the joke is that neither the jeep nor the men in it could be found. I told Sayf that it was truly funny for it was not idleness that had driven people to invent it, as he was saying, but rather a planned fabrication by the secret services. There is always a conspiracy to assassinate Nasir, sometimes from within the army, sometimes not, and thousands of people are arrested because of these alleged assassination attempts. Sayf al-Banna insisted it was a joke that people had simply made up. I told him that people were not thinking of killing Nasir, for killing an unjust ruler doesn't solve the problem. The question is much larger than killing Nasir.'

'The story of this attempt to kill Nasir in Alexandria was the subject of a discussion between you, 'Abd al-Fattah Isma'il and 'Ali 'Ashmawi. You studied its plans, its mistakes and so on!'

'What happened differs from what you say. I related Sayf's joke to 'Abd al-Fattah Isma'il. It was not studied at all for it was nothing but nonsense.'

'You also related this story to Hasan al-Hudaibi. Why? Was this too just jokes and stories that people relate?'

'Could be! Is there anything wrong with that?'

'. . . 'Abd al-'Aziz 'Ali was provisionally responsible for the *Ikhwan*'s organization until Sayyid's release from prison. Tell me, how did this happen?'

136

'This never happened!'

'How? 'Abd al-'Aziz 'Ali used to meet with 'Ali 'Ashmawi, 'Abd al-Fattah Isma'il, D'ia al-Tubji, Yahya Husain, 'Abd al-Majid al-Shadhili and Majdi 'Abd al-'Aziz. He also met Sayyid Qutb, after he was released, several times.'

'I don't know anything about these meetings.'

'Who else can know about them except you? You know very well that they did.'

'This is nothing but lies!'

'Who else worked to nominate 'Abd al-'Aziz 'Ali as the head of the organization if it was not you?'

'This is a lie!'

'What was the poison that 'Abd al-'Aziz 'Ali prepared so that Isma'il al-Fayyumi could use it against Nasir? What is the story of this poison and how did you come to agree about it?'

'You are obsessed with the idea of killing Nasir! If you really want to kill him, please kill him and give us a break! Confront me with 'Abd al-'Aziz 'Ali! Confront me with al-Hudaibi!'

'No! We'll confront you with 'Ali 'Ashmawi first!'

'Ali 'Ashmawi is a mischievous liar! I'll spit in his face because he is a venal fabricator of the truth!'

'Isn't 'Ali 'Ashmawi one of you?'

'Islam belongs only to those who are true.'

'Safwat! Bring 'Ali 'Ashmawi!'

'Ashmawi came in, still dressed in fine clothes, his hair combed back and clearly eating well.

'Ali! What happened when you went to al-Hudaibi, at the time when her leg was broken and she didn't get out of the car. You went to al-Hudaibi's daughter to ask her father's opinion?'

'Yes, that's what happened. I asked al-Hudaibi's daughter to ask her father if he fully trusted 'Abd al-'Aziz 'Ali and if he would nominate him to take over his duties. She came back to me with her father's consent for this nomination.'

'What do you say now, you B......?'

'You are a liar!', I shouted at 'Ashmawi. 'The truth is that you told me there was a brother of the *Ikhwan* who had asked for 'Abd al-'Aziz 'Ali's granddaughter's hand in marriage and who wanted to know al-Hudaibi's opinion about it all. I was then leaving my house so you, 'Ashmawi, rode with me in the car. I told you I couldn't get out of the car because of my broken leg and that it was best if you could accompany me. Al-Hudaibi's answer was that 'Abd al-'Aziz 'Ali's family was a good Muslim family and he agreed that the marriage proposal was a good one.'

'Is this the truth, 'Ali?', Shams asked.

'These are coded words and the *Hajjah* knows this very well!'

'You're a mischievous liar and your look betrays you. The *Ikhwan* are hung on posts, beaten and flogged, dogs tearing at our bodies. But you 'Ali, you are in sound condition: you are venal and cheap, a lying agent, and this is why they listen to you.'

Shams Badran instructed 'Ali to leave and then turned to me: 'Zainab! Explain to us 'Abd al-'Aziz 'Ali's link with the organization and the content of the letters exchanged between him and al-Hudaibi through you.'

'I insist that you bring 'Abd al-'Aziz 'Ali and al-Hudaibi!'

'We will.'

Instead I was made to face the wall, and neither al-Hudaibi nor 'Abd al-'Aziz 'Ali was brought.

Muhammad Qutb

'. . . What about Muhammad Qutb's organization, Zainab?'

'I have already given my answer about this subject. I told you, Muhammad Qutb did not establish any organization and that he is an Islamic writer; his job consists of showing people the right way.'

'Listen Zainab! I'm amazed that you're putting this rope around your neck. All the *Ikhwan* have saved themselves. All in all we've arrested over 100,000 people, the number still with us is 20,000. Each of these has confessed the truth, asked our pardon. We've accepted their apologies and they're now free. Even the *Murshid* Hasan al-Hudaibi, 'Abd al-Fattah Isma'il and Sayyid Qutb have confessed and apologized.

'Al-Hudaibi cursed you. Sayyid Qutb cursed you. 'Abd al-Fattah Isma'il cursed you. All the *Ikhwan* have cursed you! We admire and appreciate the stand you have taken and we deplore theirs. Forget about the swearing of the Pasha, Hamzah al-Basyuni and Safwat! We look with contempt upon the *Ikhwan* but our admiration and appreciation of you have increased. Pity that a strong personality like yours should finish in this manner. Shams Pasha is adamant about re-starting the torture, so I've assumed the task of negotiating with you so that I can go back to the Pasha with something that will save you from this predicament.

'You regularly had lunch with al-Hudaibi, by his own confession, once or twice a week at least. You used to take instructions and orders to 'Abd al-Fattah Isma'il. Give us an example of these orders. Al-Hudaibi and 'Abd al-Fattah Isma'il have confessed it. And when Sayyid Qutb was released from prison you were the liaison. We are not talking in a vacuum here.

'Madam Zainab! We have unveiled the secret of everything, all that is missing is that you cross the t's and dot the i's. Of course you will write about all this and other things too. We will report it all to Nasir and explain to him that you've changed and then refer you to the prosecution and the investigation will end. You will be released after two days and then you will be designated Social Affairs Minister, for Hikmat Abu Zayd is now the object of Nasir's anger. What do you think Madam Zainab?'

I sat at the desk and wrote the following:

In the Name of Allah, the Merciful, the Compassionate. Peace and prayers be upon the Prophet, his family and Companions. I praise Allah and thank Him, even though I cannot offer Him thanks that befit His glory, may He be exalted. He has chosen me - without any merit of mine - to be on the path that He has chosen for His servants: the path of the Qur'an and the *Sunnah*, the path of truth to which He called all humanity. (*O mankind! There has come to you a direction from your Lord and a healing for the (diseases) in your hearts . . .*),[2] (*O you people! Adore your Guardian-Lord Who created you and those who came before you . . .*)[3] Praise be to Allah that He has made me stand underneath the banner of (*Our Lord! We have heard the call of one calling (us) to Faith, 'Believe in your Lord', and we have believed . . .*).[4] Praise be to Allah Who made me stand underneath the umbrella of: (*Allah has purchased of the believers their persons and their goods; for theirs (in return) is Paradise . . .*).[5] And Praise be to Him that He has chosen me from among believing men and believing women and selected me for the company of believing men and women so that we witness Allah's message, which we have devoted our lives to spreading and calling people towards with every dear and valuable thing we have in order to achieve what Allah has said in the Qur'an: (*Allah has purchased of the believers their persons and their goods; for theirs (in return) is Paradise: they fight in His cause and slay and are slain . . .*) and (*You are the best of people, evolved for mankind, enjoining what is right, forbidding what is wrong . . .*).[6]

With all that, I repeat and stress that we are still on the path of witnessing that 'there is no god but

Allah, without associating anyone with Him, and Muhammad is His Messenger', and still adhering to both parts of the *shahadah*: guardians of Allah's Book, safekeeping its commandments and laws and calling for (*We have sent down to you the Book in truth, that you might judge between men as guided by Allah . . .*).[7] We are the Prophet's trustees and this religion's trustees too. O Allah! Be witness that we are still firm on the way, neither changing nor altering. Help us defeat every transgressor who associates others with You, becomes an enemy to Your Religion and fights Your Book and the defenders of Your Prophet. O Allah! It is with this that I live and with it I will stand in front of You. So accept me as one of the people of *Tawhid*: the people of the true word who fear You and worship You correctly. O Allah! Provide me with the gift of loving for Your sake, despising for Your sake and making *Jihad* for Your sake!

This is my way, people, so do what you like and wish! I will call people to Allah with enlightenment, therefore do not bother trying to reach us with your shortcomings and plunge us into the darkness of disbelief and association of other things with Allah and your fight against Islam and its people. We wash our hands of you and your deeds and we are confronting your falsehood until we meet Allah.

Signed Zainab al-Ghazali

'What is this?', stormed Shams as he read what I had written. 'Safwat, give her a thousand floggings! The woman has mocked us all! She is laughing at us all with her cunning. The B......... is more than an orator!

'The doctors have said that you're about to die, but it's necessary that you go to court to hear with your own ears the death sentence which will be pronounced against you.

141

Your punishment for what your hands have sown. We'll send you to the prosecution tomorrow morning. And know that if you don't give in the prosecution will return you to us.'

The Case for the Prosecution

And now the prosecution. The final scene of the comedy, where innocent people are punished under the auspices of justice and sovereignty of the law.

I went inside the tent where the investigators awaited me. It is all one plan that they are executing. In these tents, the investigators continued to threaten the accused, to put pressure on them to sign whatever they wrote, even though it was all lies and slander. All this in front of judges and legal advisers especially assigned to supervise the hearings.

The prosecuting attorney looked at my exhausted state, with bandages around my feet, and my voice barely audible. He sat behind a heap of files and dictated to his secretary my name, age, place of birth and address.

Then, turning towards me, he said: 'Zainab! In these files and dossiers are the *Ikhwan*'s confessions, your position in them is clear. I want the truth from you. This is the truth confessed by Hasan al-Hudaibi, Sayyid Qutb, 'Abd al-Fattah Isma'il and all the other members of the *Ikhwan*. I want you, Zainab, to forget your obstinacy and stop wasting our time in what does not bring any benefit to anyone.'

He asked me a number of questions, which I answered, but I was surprised to see that he wrote a whole page of notes to each answer when I said only a few words in response. I was extremely unhappy about this.

'What's going on Mr. Qannawi? I have answered your questions with only a few words, so why all this writing?'

'I'm helping you, Zainab, for each word that I write will be shown to the President. He has asked to see your confessions, in particular, on a daily basis.'

'That's of no concern to me! What I'm concerned about is that my name is attributed only to what I say.'

'I will read everything to you later!'

'What's the point so long as you're writing what you want. There's no need for me to speak. But let me tell you, I will never admit, should there be a court hearing, to anything that I have not said.'

'You have said that Nasir is a *kafir* and that his government is a *kafir* government and that society is also *kafir*.'

'We don't say that the people of the *Qiblah* are *kafirs*!'

'Who are the people of the *Qiblah*?'

'Those who say: "There is no god but Allah and Muhammad is His Messenger" and then adhere to what the Prophet (peace be upon him) brought from His Lord.'

'Explain to me the characteristics of the "people of the *Qiblah*".'

'They are those who pray, give *Zakat*, fast during Ramadan, perform *Hajj* if they can, and adhere to the commandments of the Qur'an and the *Sunnah*. They don't legislate anything themselves, and do not take as their laws anything but that which Allah has revealed.'

'Do you consider Nasir, his government and society to be "people of the *Qiblah*"?'

'Nasir as such, no, for he is a ruler who could rule with Allah's Book if he wanted to, but instead he works to impede it. He is legislating for people things from himself and obstructs Allah's Book. Besides, Nasir has said that he does not want to establish a religious state.'

'I want you to frankly tell me your opinion: Are Nasir and his government *kafirs* or not?'

'I have already answered you and whoever wants to know his position *vis-à-vis* Allah, let him apply himself to Allah's Book.'

By this time, the prosecuting attorney had written five pages.

'Zainab, you wanted to kill Umm Kulthum and 'Abd al-Halim Hafiz!'[8]

'Those who are busy in calling others to the religion of Allah and the return of the Muslim *ummah* cannot be bothered about such futile things. When Muslims consciously return to their religion, all these depravities will end and the Muslim *ummah* will rid us of this hateful loosening of manners, and of Satan's worship which takes different forms and which caused the collapse of the *ummah* and brought it down to such a low point.'

In this way, the prosecuting attorney continued for ten days. Writing his copious notes, notes which documented everything other than what I had said. He asked me to sign what he had written but I refused. The comedy of investigation over, he sent me back to the torturous grip of Shams Badran to be flogged anew.

More Torture

Two days later I was, once again, recalled by the prosecution. This time a number of our youth who had been severely tortured were also present.

'When did you meet them? When did you get to know them? What are their names?', Qannawi asked me.

I asked my brothers: 'When did I see you? Did you really meet me? What are your names?'

The prosecuting attorney then shouted in protest, claiming that I was directing them with my own questions. So I told him to ask them himself when they'd met me. This he did to which each and every one answered that they'd never met me!

'But you each said during your interrogation that you had!'

'Under the clutches of their tortures, we said just anything.'

This charade, as they dragged in more young men and repeated the same line of questioning to the same effect, continued day after day.

Repeatedly I was returned to Shams Badran and frequently from there to hospital.

'Zainab Ghazali! Explain your contacts with Khalidah Hudaibi and her husband Ahmad Thabit and their roles in the *Ikhwan*.'

'The joint activities of myself and Khalidah al-Hudaibi, were confined to helping the families of those imprisoned.'

'What kind of help?'

'Financial help or help in kind.'

I then explained that help in kind consisted of materials, semolina, wheat, rice, beans and butter.

When asked about Khalidah Hudaibi's husband Ahmad Thabit, I explained that he only came to the Muslim Ladies' Headquarters to collect the things I sent to his wife so that they could be handed over to needy families. He did not even leave his car as our people brought the things out for him. But Shams did not believe me and handed me over to Safwat and his dogs.

'. . . We've brought al-Zayni from Ghazah. The *Murshid* and Ma'mun al-Hudaibi have identified him. It is he who brought you money and if you don't identify him we'll restart investigations with you from the beginning. Do you understand? What's important is that al-Zayni has confessed everything!'

I was taken to a room where a man was sitting in such a way that it was impossible to identify him.

'Who is this?', Shams Badran asked.

'I do not know him!', I replied.

'Everyone has recognized him, he's Sadiq al-Zayni, you B.........!'

Jalal al-Dib intervened to ask about the money. I explained again that it was for needy families: for their food, clothing, schooling, and medical treatment. It was for the families of the lions behind bars.

'Throw her to snakes not dogs!', screamed Shams.

'Zainab! I will relate two events that you were involved in. One involving Muhammad Qutb, al-Hudaibi's wife and Muhammad Qutb's sisters and another involving 'Ali 'Ashmawi and Ma'mun al-Hudaibi. I am telling you things which have been related to us by Hasan al-Hudaibi, his wife and Muhammad Qutb, and we want you to confirm them.

'One day you phoned Muhammad Qutb, who came to see you at night from Halwan. You gave him your jewellery and a further E£500. You told him to give the money to "mother" - meaning al-Hudaibi's wife - and that your jewellery was to help needy families. You asked him to keep them and give them to the respected mother when the time was right.'

'Yes, this happened, and what of it? It's my jewellery, and mine to give as I please. And I indeed did give it to the best people: to the *Ikhwan*, to help suffering families. As for the money, it belonged to the *Ikhwan* and I gave it back because I was afraid that something might happen to it.'

'The E£500 was for the "organization" not for the families.'

'No, it was for the families!'

''Ali 'Ashmawi said it was for the organization.'

''Ali 'Ashmawi is a liar!'

'Muhammad Qutb said that he didn't know what the money was for, you just told him to take it, along with your jewellery, and to hand it over to al-Hudaibi's wife.'

'Then bring Muhammad Qutb here, for I told him that the E£500 was to help the needy families.'

'Well! Where did this E£500 come from?'

'One day, 'Ali 'Ashmawi came to me requesting written permission for a brother from Saudi Arabia to meet the *Murshid* or Ma'mun. I told him that Brother Ma'mun needed no go-between and that the *Murshid* was in Alexandria. Nevertheless, Ma'mun was available and he could meet him. 'Ali 'Ashmawi came back later and informed me that the brother had met Ma'mun and donated this sum and that Ma'mun had asked that this money be brought to me. According to what 'Ali 'Ashmawi said, the brother from Saudi Arabia requested him to give me the money.'

'This money was not for these families, for Muhammad Qutb has said otherwise.'

'I am the only one able to state the truth. Muhammad Qutb may have confused the matter, if he has really said as you claim.'

At last, Muhammad Qutb was brought in and explained that he had been given the money and jewellery so that he could take them to the respected mother. I tried to remind him about what I had said, namely that the money was for the families and that it had been given to me in trust, but, sadly, he could not remember. Yet, he did add that if I said the money was for the families, then what I said must be true.

'. . . Zainab, tell us about the organization established by Muhammad Qutb.'

'I've already answered this question. Muhammad Qutb did not establish any organization.'

'Safwat, suspend her!'

'Give us information about Muhammad Qutb. We'll remember this favour and reach an agreement with you which is to your advantage.'

'How could I reach an agreement with you? I despise your ways and your falsehood! You're nothing but Satan's

agents, you'll never succeed in making us betray each
other. We are the Merciful's servants! None of us will
implicate his brothers no matter how much you try your
tricks and manoeuvres!'

'If you don't tell us you'll be flogged again, and the
prosecution will investigate you anew.'

'The prosecution is with you and at your service. None
of you knows Allah's way, you are among the people
who went astray, whom Allah is angry with.'

The following morning, I was taken to Riyad Ibrahim's
office. He asked me about the people I had met from
Kardasah.

'I don't know anything about Kardasah!'

'Didn't you meet anybody from there?'

'No!'

'Ahmad 'Abd al-Majid is from Kardasah!'

Minced Meat

The doctors diagnozed that my health had deteriorated
so much, I would die if not allowed wholesome food. If
my condition did not improve I would not be able to
stand trial. For this reason, I was permitted food from
outside, but only fruit and curdled milk.

One day, however, my sister managed to bring in some
meat: she had emptied a box of dried milk and filled it
with minced meat, curdled milk and oranges. At the time
no-one realized what was in it, including myself. I took
my share and gave the rest to Nurse 'Abd al-Ma'bud to
distribute to other sick members of the *Ikhwan* in hospital.
The nurse took it and left, but quickly returned: 'This will
do you good *Hajjah*, it's minced meat!'

I begged him to give each of the sick a spoonful of it.
So he did, but nevertheless came back with some he had

held back for me. I asked him to take it to 'Abd al-'Aziz
'Ali, the ex-Minister of Municipalities, along with a box of
curdled milk. The latter, curious to know where the food
had come from, learned that it was from my cell and he
thanked Allah.

Each of the *Ikhwan* would save, as I had, from the little
they had in order to help their brothers. Nearly a year
had elapsed since I had been arrested and I was only
allowed food from outside three months before my trial.
Even more hideous was the fact that I learned during a
visit by my mother and sister only days before the trial
began that Safwat al-Rubi had asked them, from the early
days of my arrest, to send large quantities of medicines,
fruit and clothes. He had further insisted that all the
clothes should be new.

It was a malicious plan to drain the resources of the
mujahidin, by over-burdening our families outside. They
wanted to give the people allowed into their courts the
impression that their treatment of the accused had been
as good as they could possibly achieve and that they had
our well-being at heart.

Salah's Repentance

Even in this bleak, dark dungeon, dear reader, there
was the occasional occurrence, albeit rare, which restored
one's faith in humanity, in humanity's love for good. May
Allah be exalted!

In our military hospital, there was a soldier-nurse by
the name of Salah whose job it was to administer injections
and to generally watch the cells. On my way to the toilet
one day, the wind lifted the blanket which acted as the
door to Sayyid Qutb's cell and, by sheer chance, I caught
a glimpse of Sayyid Qutb. The hospital was immediately
in an uproar, for Qutb was not allowed to be seen by
other prisoners, and a fluke chance was no excuse. Salah

began cursing and swearing, and what made the incident even more contentious was that Safwat al-Rubi happened to enter the hospital at that very moment; the soldiers wanted to impress him, demonstrate their alacrity in following orders.

Salah became like an enraged beast void of humanity, reason or *din*. But somehow Sayyid Qutb managed to appease him, make him understand that he had nothing to do with the blanket lifting. Gradually, Salah was soothed, his new-found calm ensuring the matter would not be reported.

Remarkably, a few days later Salah came to me saying he wished to renew his faith in Islam, and asking how a true Muslim behaved.

'Can you bear what you see happening to the *Ikhwan*?', I asked him.

'If I become a Muslim the way they are Muslims, then Allah will give me patience and strength.'

'Repeat "There is no god but Allah and Muhammad is the Messenger of Allah".'

This he did, so I then advised: 'Don't do anything except that which Allah orders you to do. Don't obey the despots if by obeying them you disobey Allah.'

'I want to understand real Islam, the Islam that has enabled you to endure all this torture in such a patient manner and in a way that no human should be expected to do so!'

I suggested he talk with Professor Sayyid Qutb and ask him to explain these things as Salah administered his injections. I further sent him with greetings to my dear brother!

The Day of the Trial Draws Near

Many days passed before I received the prosecuting attorney's petition informing me of the trial date. It was a scandal second to none. For we had been informed that the courts were, in any case, in Shams Badran's pocket. We were denied the right to defend ourselves and meet lawyers, and when I asked for Ahmad al-Khawajah as defence attorney, I was told it was not permitted. Instead a Christian lawyer was to defend me. My family was allowed to visit me before the trial began. My mother and my two sisters came along but were clearly devastated when they saw how weak I had become. I did my best to cheer them up whilst we sat in the presence of Safwat and Hamzah al-Basyuni. I requested my relatives not to ask any lawyer to defend me, but was informed that they had already hired Husain Abu Zayd for a fee of E£1000, half of which was to be paid before the trial and the other half upon completion. I begged them not to proceed with this arrangement but to no avail.

The day before the trial, I was taken to Shams Badran's office.

'You're requested', he advised, 'not to object to anything mentioned in the minutes of the investigations and to endorse every word mentioned therein. If you apologize to the court and say that the *Ikhwan* have cheated you and if you demonstrate remorse for what you have done, the court will pass a lenient sentence. Be careful not to oppose any word mentioned in the investigations. If you decide to wash your hands of the *Ikhwan*, you will find us most helpful.'

'Allah does what He wills and chooses. (*It is not fitting for a believer, man or woman, when a matter has been decided by Allah and His Apostle, to have any option about their decision . . .*)[9]

'Speak in Arabic, not in gibberish. It seems that you are set against helping yourself.'

'(*With Him are the keys of the unseen, the treasures that none knows but He. He knows whatever there is on the earth and in the sea. Not a leaf falls but with His knowledge: there is not a grain in the darkness (or depths) of the earth, nor anything fresh or dry (green or withered) but is (inscribed) in a clear record (to those who can read).)'*[10]

'Take her Hamzah, she is free to consider, or not consider, her benefit.'

I began thinking about these despots and the court's readiness to do whatever they asked. I could not understand - when all were in their hands - their desire to prevent us speaking in court or changing what they had written in the minutes. It seemed to me, dear reader, that their theatrical play had not come to an end, at least not without the charade at court. They wanted to display us, saying: 'Look! These are the *Ikhwan* who wanted to kill the President and who have confessed trying to do so.' But Allah will ensure they are disappointed, their hopes will come to nothing and their scandalous games will be exposed.

Glad Tidings

In the exuberance of all this, I had a vision: standing in a court I was told it was about to pronounce its judgement upon us. But suddenly, the walls of this court vanished and instead I found myself standing in a huge yard the surface of which was earth. Then heaven fell on earth as a tent would fall to the ground. Light filled the whole earth, a light linking heaven to earth. I saw the Prophet (peace be upon him) standing in front of me in the direction of the *Qiblah.* I was behind him and I heard him say: 'Listen Zainab to the voice of truth.' Together we heard a voice which reached both the heavens and earth, saying: 'Here the courts of falsehood will be held and the despots' sentences will be issued unjustly and unduly against you. You are the trust's holders and leaders of the way (... *persevere in patience and constancy; vie in such perseverance;*

strengthen each other, and fear Allah, that you may prosper).'[11]

When the voice stopped, I looked at the Prophet (peace be upon him) who pointed to the right. I looked and saw a rope which reached up to heaven, but it was more like a carpet covered with green grass. The Prophet (peace be upon him) said to me: 'Zainab! Climb this mountain and you will find at its zenith Hasan al-Hudaibi. Tell him these words', and he looked at me in such a way that it overtook my whole being. The Prophet (peace be upon him) did not utter any audible words but I understood what he wanted from me. Then the Prophet (peace be upon him) lifted his hand towards the mountain and I found myself climbing it. As I was climbing, I met Khalidah and 'Aliyah al-Hudaibi on the way and I asked them: 'Are you with us on the way?'

'Yes.'

I left them and continued climbing. Within a few metres, I met Aminah and Hamidah Qutb with Fatimah 'Isa. I asked them too: 'Are you with us on the way?'

'Yes!', came their reply.

I continued climbing until I reached the top of the mountain where I found a plain surface in the middle of which was a court furnished with rugs, sofas and pillows and al-Hudaibi sitting in the middle. When al-Hudaibi saw me, he stood up and greeted me, clearly happy to see me.

'I am sent by the Prophet [peace be upon him] to deliver to you a few words as a trust from him, a trust which is on the Prophet, may peace be on him', I said as we shook hands.

He explained that he had already received it, praise be to Allah. And we sat as these words were transmitted through our souls, inaudible in any other way. Sitting with al-Hudaibi I looked to the bottom of the mountain where I saw two naked women on a train. I, painfully, notified al-Hudaibi who also looked at the train, saying: 'Do you oppose them?'

'Yes!'

'Do you think that what we have attained is due to us and our efforts? It is rather because of the grace of Allah, so don't busy yourself with them.'

'We have to resist in order to bring them to the right path!'

'Can you do this by yourself?'

'By Allah!'

'Let's praise Allah for what He has given us.'

He raised his hands as if thanking Allah, as I did too. As we repeated our thanks to Allah I woke up.

The feeling which now came over me was one of unencumbered peace, rest and tranquillity. This vision had washed away all my pain and driven away all the fear and sorrow in my heart (. . . *those who have left their homes, or been driven out therefrom, or suffered harm in My cause, or fought or been slain, - verily, I will blot out from them their iniquities, and admit them into gardens with rivers flowing beneath; - a reward from the Presence of Allah, and from His Presence is the best of rewards. Let not the strutting about of the unbelievers through the land deceive you . . . O you who believe! Persevere in patience and constancy; vie in such perseverance; strengthen each other and fear Allah; that you may prosper*).[12]

Judgement Day

On the day of the trial we were taken to the court in lorries. Lorries packed tight because of the sheer number of soldiers, officers and policemen that escorted us. Once there we were put in a single cage. We were 43 in number:

Sayyid Qutb Ibrahim
Muhammad Yusuf Hawash
'Abd al-Fattah 'Abduh Isma'il

Ahmad 'Abd al-Majid 'Abd al-Sami'
Sabri 'Arafah Ibrahim al-Kumi
Majdi 'Abd al-'Aziz Mutwalli
'Abd al-Majid Yusuf 'Abd al-Majid Mutwalli
'Abbas Sa'id al-Sisi
Mubarak 'Abd al-Adim Mahmud 'Ayad
Faruq Ahmad 'Ali al-Manshawi
Fayiz Muhammad Isma'il Yusuf
Mamduh Darwish Mustafa al-Diri
Muhammad Ahmad Muhammad 'Abd al-Rahman
Jalal al-Din Bakri Dissawi
Muhammad 'Abd al-Mu'ti Ibrahim al-Jazzar
Muhammad al-Ma'mun Yahya Zakaria
Ahmad 'Abd al-Halim al-Saruji
Salah Muhammad Muhammad Khalifah
al-Sayyid Sa'd al-Din al-Sayyid Sharif
Muhammad 'Abd al-Mu'ti 'Abd al-Rahim
Imam 'Abd al-Latif 'Abd al-Fattah Ghayth
Kamal 'Abd al-'Aziz al-'Urfi Salam
Fu'ad Hasan 'Ali Mutawalli
Muhammad Ahmad al-Buhayri
Hamdi Hasan Salah
Mustafa 'Abd al-'Aziz al-Khudayri
al-Sayyid Nazili Muhammad 'Awdiyah.
Mursi Mustafa Mursi
Muhammad Badi' 'Abd al-Majid Muhammad Sami
Muhammad 'Abd al-Min'im Shahin
Mahmud Ahmad Fakhri
Mahmud 'Izzat Ibrahim
Salah Muhammad 'Abd al-Haq
Hilmi Muhammad Sadiq Hathut
Ilham Yahya 'Abd al-Majid Badawi
'Abd al-Mun'im 'Abd al-Ra'uf Yusuf 'Arafat
Muhammad 'Abd al-Fattah Rizq Sharif
Zainab al-Ghazali al-Jubaili
Hamidah Qutb Ibrahim

Muhyi al-din Hilal
'Ashmawi Sulaiman
Mustafa al-'Alim

If you trouble, dear reader, to count these entries you will note only 42 names. For our number was only completed by 'Ali 'Ashmawi who had been admitted as an approver, and had thus sold his *din*. What a humiliation!

As we entered the cage, al-Dajawi called our names one after the other, asking each of us: 'Do you have any objections about the court?'

Each in turn replied: 'I have no objection about the individuals as such, but I do object to the law by which we are judged, because it is a *Jahili* law and we do not accept as our legislation anything except Allah's legislation.'

Al-Dajawi then read: 'The court has decided that Zainab al-Ghazali and Hamidah Qutb be judged by a special trial.'

The two of us were taken out and placed in a room until the session ended, and from there, back to the Military prison.

This happened on 10th April 1966. We were to remain in our cells until 17th May 1966 when a further mock trial would take place.

Notes and References

1. *Al-Tawbah*: 111.

2. *Yunus*: 57.

3. *Al-Baqarah*: 21.

4. *Al 'Imran*: 193.

5. *Al-Tawbah*: 111.

6. *Al 'Imran*: 110.

7. *Al-Nisa'*: 105.

8. Two famous Egyptian singers.

9. *Al-Ahzab*: 36.

10. *Al-An'am*: 59.

11. *Al 'Imran*: 200.

12. *Ibid.*: 195-200.

CHAPTER 6

In Court

I returned to court on 17th May 1966 and was promptly placed in the cage. The court consisted of the pompous al-Dajawi and members of the prosecution, who sat on his right. A number of journalists sat around a small table, having taken their photographs of the accused. Among these was 'Abd al-'Azim who had previously covered the activities of the Muslim Ladies Group. I addressed him: 'Abd al-'Azim! Keep these photographs, we may need them one day, and who knows, maybe that day will be very soon.'

'Alright!', he was courageous enough to reply, but meanwhile he trembled and his face became pale. A few minutes later he had gone from the court.

Al-Dajawi began the court's deliberations by calling me to the bar to answer questions. Nothing he asked me had anything to do with what I had said during the investigations. To every question, I replied: 'I did not say this during investigation!'

But to draw your attention to the falsehoods they described, I will relate just two questions that I did answer: 'Hasan al-Hudaibi said that you stole the E£4,000 that you gave him from your husband.'

'The E£4,000 that I gave him was the *Ikhwan*'s membership fees and donations. It was to be spent on

159

the families of the imprisoned that Nasir displaced after the 1954 trials, and this is what I said under investigation.'

Al-Dajawi panicked, trembled as if bitten by a snake, then asked: 'At the time when your leg was broken, you were very scared that something might happen to this money. Why? And when 'Abd al-Fattah Isma'il came to see you in hospital, you told him to take the money from the safe in your house and hand it over to al-Hudaibi. Why?'

'Because it was the money of Islamic *Da'wah*: the rights of the *Mujahidin* you imprisoned and whose families you displaced. Had I died my inheritors would have received property which did not belong to me. It is *da'wah* property.'

'It was intended for the procurement of arms, Madam, and Al-Hudaibi has said that he knew of no other source from which this money could have come except you taking it from your husband', the prosecuting attorney interrupted.

'This never happened!', I quickly interjected.

'Does Al-Hudaibi lie?'

'God forbid!'

The prosecuting attorney then responded with a barrage of foul language. I was surprised, for I did not expect to hear such language in front of a court. Had the despot killed off all manners and dignity in Egypt?

Al-Dajawi finished his questioning of me, and I was returned to the cage. The prosecution's speech followed. Again, a barrage of the most despicable, base language, slandering and defamating innocent people's honour.

I felt myself becoming more and more upset because of all the falsehood incarnated in the court. I raised my hand requesting permission to speak. Al-Dajawi - who foolishly believed himself to be a real judge - thought that I wanted to apologize for fear of their falsehood and for fear of their threats and their demands that I be sentenced to death; a life sentence was not enough to punish me for my crimes, they said. Al-Dajawi looked at me, ignorance encompassing his face, and allowed me to speak:

'In the Name of Allah, the Merciful, the Compassionate! We are the trustees of an *ummah* and the inheritors of a Book and the guardians of a *Shari'ah*. We have in the Prophet (peace be upon him) a good example (*Uswah*) and we stand firm on the way till we raise the banner of "there is no god but Allah". Allah is Sufficient unto us and He is the best Disposer of affairs for what the unjust have fabricated against us.'

I pointed to the prosecution and the court representatives and repeated: 'Allah is Sufficient unto us and He is the best Disposer of affairs for all this falsehood, slander and sin.'

Al-Dajawi shouted hysterically: 'Shut up! Shut up! What is she saying? What does *Uswah* mean? What does this word mean?'

And, as he repeated 'What does this word mean?', everyone in the courtroom burst into laughter at the man assigned as judge but who did not understand *Uswah*. Thus did Nasir choose his men. Could the assistants of losers be but losers? I sat down, saying: 'Ignorance is but a cause of corruption and brings every kind of evil deed with it. Let history be a witness as to who is ruling and judging us.'

The session was concluded. I was returned to the prison and made to pay dearly for what I had said.

Greater Jahiliyyah

Again I was called for investigation in the prison. Again, I was asked about certain people, and each time I said I did not know them I was tortured and made to stand against the wall. This despite the fact that my trial had supposedly ended. Did such a thing ever happen during any other inquisition or trial in history? Did such a thing ever happen even at the beginning of *da'wah* of the Prophet (peace be upon him), during the time of the darkness of the Quraysh?

By God, no! and history is a witness to that.

Judgement is Pronounced

At last, the day came on which our sentences were to be pronounced. We were taken, Hamidah and I, to court in a lorry, behind another lorry carrying our brothers.

We were made to sit in a room and wait until the men had been sentenced. Then to a room where an officer was sitting. He called my name and said: 'Zainab al-Ghazali al-Jubaili is sentenced to 25 years hard labour with the seizure of all confiscated items.'

'Allah is Greater and all praise is due to Him. It is for the sake of Allah and the call of truth: the call of Islam (*So lose not heart, nor fall into despair: for you must gain mastery if you are true in Faith*).'[1]

He then called Hamidah Qutb, and said: 'Ten Years hard labour.'

I hugged her, while repeating: 'Allah is Greater and to Him is all praise. It is for the sake of a state based on the teachings of the Qur'an, God willing.'

We repeated our faith until we arrived at the court jail. We were anxious, awaiting reassurance about our brothers' sentences. As soon as they saw us, they shouted: 'So what happened sister Zainab?'

'Twenty-five years hard labour for the sake of the Islamic state that is governed by the Qur'an and the *Sunnah*, God willing.'

'And sister Hamidah?'

'Ten years hard labour for the sake of Allah and the *da'wah* of Islam.'

I asked about the sentences of Sayyid Qutb, 'Abd al-Fattah Isma'il, Yusuf Hawash and the rest. They informed me that they were to be martyrs for the sake of Allah. By this I understood they had been sentenced to death. I reiterated: 'O Allah! Accept them as martyrs for the sake of the state of Islam that rules by the Qur'an and the *Sunnah*, God willing.'

Safwat al-Rubi along with a number of soldiers forced Hamidah and I into another, smaller, lorry. Journalists tried to take photographs of us but I rushed towards them intending to smash their cameras, shouting: 'O you who applaud every transgressor! O you who consume ill-gotten properties at the despots' tables, what are you doing?'

When we reached the military prison I was again punished for what I had said.

From the day our sentences were pronounced, Hamidah and I were put in the same cell.

Moments in Allah's Pleasure

Five days after we had been sentenced, Sayyid Qutb, accompanied by the chief of the prison, Ibrahim and Safwat al-Rubi, came to our cell. Ibrahim then left, leaving us with Sayyid Qutb and Safwat.

'Welcome Brother Sayyid', I said. 'This is a happy, pleasant surprise. The moments that you spend with us are moments spent in Allah's pleasure.'

Sayyid Qutb talked with us about life's decrees and their timing, explaining these were controlled only by Allah. He asked us to submit and delegate our affairs to Allah. We also spoke about accepting Allah's decrees. He then whispered a few words of encouragement to his sister and a few to me. However, by this time Safwat was becoming impatient and angry and he declared that it was time for Sayyid Qutb to leave.

The *Imam, Shahid* Sayyid Qutb looked at us, saying: 'Let's not bother and let's get ourselves used to patience!'

He then said his farewells and left.

The Last Bargain

The night prior to Sayyid's execution, the despots tried to persuade Hamidah to intervene on behalf of her brother. I will let her relate what happened. She said: 'Hamzah al-Basyuni called me to his office and showed me the death sentence decree and its endorsement, saying: "The government is ready to lessen the sentence if your brother consents to do what it asks of him. Your brother is not only a loss to you but to Egypt too. I cannot imagine that we are going to lose such a man in only a few hours. Our aim is to save him however we can. All he has to say is a few words to save himself from death. And none can have more impact on him than you. You are the only person who can convey this message to him. Remember, just a few words is all he has to say and everything will be over. We want him to explain that this movement was in contact with a certain party and, if he does, then he'll be released for health reasons".'

'But you know as well as Nasir does that this movement has nothing to do with any party or country', I replied.

'I know, and everyone knows that you are the only people in Egypt who work for *'aqidah*. We know that you are the best people in the country but, at this moment, we want to save Sayyid Qutb from execution.'

'If you want to convey this to him I don't mind!'

He asked Safwat to take me to my brother, and once in his cell I relayed our conversation to him. He looked at me to see behind the intent of what I said, as if asking: 'Is it you who is asking this or them?'

I managed to make him understand by gestures that it was they who wanted this from him.

'By Allah! Had this been true, I would have said it and no power on earth would stop me from saying it. But it did not happen and I will never tell a lie', was his response.

'You mean this is your decision!', yelled Safwat.

'Yes!'

Safwat then left us, saying: 'You can stay together for a while!'

I then explained the whole story to Sayyid, telling him it was Hamzah who had called me and showed me the death sentence decree and had asked me to convey the message.

'And you', he asked, 'would you have liked me to say what they wanted?'

'No!'

'They possess neither good nor harm for themselves. Life decrees are in the hands of Allah. These despots can neither prolong nor shorten my life. All is in the hands of Allah, and Allah is behind us encompassing everything.'

The Executions

A few days later, we heard that the death sentences on *Imam Shahid* Sayyid Qutb, *Shahid* 'Abd al-Fattah Isma'il and *Shahid* Yusuf Hawash had been carried out. News of the executions fell on us like a dead weight, for those executed were all dear, good *mujahids*. How was I to console Sayyid's sister? How was I to comfort her? What could I possibly do? Rather, how was I to console myself and find comfort in all this calamity?

Such a great loss. Sayyid Qutb, the *mufassir* (exegete) of the Qur'an and Islamic *Da'iyah*, a sage in his understanding, eloquence, clarity, and force of argument. A man who held fast to his religion, trusting in Allah's victory. The author of the great *tafsir Fi zilal al-Qur'an*, which ushered in a new era of reflecting and pondering over the Qur'an, the Book of Allah, a new way of understanding His commandments, has shown what real adherence to *din* is.

Sayyid Qutb had shown this unique way in the

Introduction to the *tafsir* of *Surah al-An'am*. Sayyid Qutb, the author of *Hadha al-Din, Al-'Adalah al-Ijtima'iyah fi al-Islam, Al-Mustaqbal li hadha al-Din, Al-Taswir al-fanni fi al-Qur'an, Mashahid al-qiyama fi al-Qur'an* and another 20 or so books in every field of the sciences of the Qur'an.

Words do not console at the time of such events! Read the *ma'alim* to find out why Sayyid was executed! Sayyid Qutb even forecast Islamic resurgence in the lands of both superpowers. That meant the end of these superpowers, one day, and the establishment of the rule of Islam in order to abolish *Jahili* anarchy. Indeed, the rise of Islam means the establishment of the only legal power which has the right to govern this world (. . . *the best of people, evolved for mankind* . . .)[2] so that (. . . *Allah will complete (the revelation of) His light, even though the unbelievers may detest (it)).*[3]

Last Days in the Military Prison

On the day of Sayyid's execution, I dozed after *Fajr* prayer and saw him in a dream.

'Know that I was not with them, I was in Madinah in the company of the Prophet (peace be upon him)', he said.

I woke and immediately informed Hamidah.

The following day, I again dozed after *Fajr* prayer while reading the supplication of the concluding prayer, and heard a voice saying: 'Sayyid is in the highest *Firdaus*[4] and his companions are in '*Iliyin*.'[5]

I woke and related the same to Hamidah who cried, saying: 'I am sure of Allah's favour on us and that, God willing, Sayyid is in the highest *Firdaus*.'

'These visions are consolation, a strengthening from Allah, the Exalted, the High.'

More executions were carried out and all the while we faced hardships such as people can barely endure. The impudent continued to call me to their offices, leaving

Hamidah alone and a prey for pain, worry and fearful waiting. I would return and tell her about the new Muslims arrested by the despots, more victims they asked me about. These persecutors wanted to incriminate me anew, a life sentence was not enough for them!

So we lived in the military prison, under constant threat, in the evil shadow of their torture. Yet, we continued to find in the Qur'an the best of dwellings, so we lived truthfully with it. Allah spoke truly when He said: (. . . *for without doubt in the remembrance of Allah do hearts find satisfaction*).[6] We asked the prison authorities to allow us newspapers and magazines. Hamzah al-Basyuni promised to bring them at the expense of other allowances. We agreed and so the cruelty of being cut off diminished and we were once again linked with news of people outside!

My Husband's Death

The day I was sentenced, I made a request via Hamzah al-Basyuni to see my husband. When he did not come, I repeated my request. I was called to their offices and asked the reason for my insistence.

'I have been sentenced to 25 years and want to inform my husband that I am releasing him from the bonds of our marriage, so that he may be free to do what he likes.'

'Nasir will do it. He didn't sentence you to death but he will gradually kill you anyway!', was Hamzah's harsh response.

'Allah is the Doer. Nasir, you and the whole world together cannot make a leaf fall from a tree except by Allah's permission.'

'We will bring your divorce decree shortly.'

'You are nothing but beasts.'

Back in my cell, cruel days went by until once again I was reading the Qur'an after *Fajr* when I dozed off. In a dream I saw my husband's picture in the deceased column of the newspaper. I woke, saying: 'O Allah! We don't ask You to take back decrees but ask You to bring benevolence with these decrees.'

I was surprised to hear Hamidah repeating the same *du'a*, but did not tell her what I had seen in my dream. I had this same dream often after that.

Then, one Friday morning, as I read the newspapers, I came upon my husband's photograph in the deceased person's column. 'There is no god but Allah and Muhammad is His Bondsman and Messenger. (. . . *to Allah we belong and to Him is our return.*)[7] To Paradise, God willing, Haj Muhammad!', I said before bursting into tears and passing out.

Shortly afterwards, my family came to see me. They informed me that Nasir and his soldiers had given my good, righteous husband, al-Haj Muhammad Salim Salim two choices: either divorce Zainab al-Ghazali al-Jubaili or be taken to the military prison. He requested two weeks to think about it, but they forced him to make a choice there and then. Amongst the soldiers who had gone to my husband was Abu al-Wafa Danqal who had taken the *Ma'zun*[8] with him, so that he could issue an act of divorce against me.

My husband signed what they wanted, saying: 'O Allah! Be witness that I have not divorced my wife Zainab al-Ghazali al-Jubaili. I'm going to die, so let me die in dignity. I shall die while she is still under the bonds of our marriage.'

My husband had suffered a partial paralysis when they had sentenced me to 25 years hard labour. Prior to that he had *angina pectoris*, the result of Nasir having seized all his wealth, factories, housing and lands. Allah is Sufficient unto us and He is the best Disposer of affairs. My husband died shortly after signing the divorce act. When my family heard that he had consented to the divorce, they removed his photograph from the living room. But upon hearing this I too became angry and asked that the photograph be put back exactly where it was. For my husband was a brother in Allah before being a husband, and my house will remain his as long as I live. *'Aqidah* had bound us together before marriage had. Besides, marriage is only a contingent worldly event, but brotherhood in Allah is everlasting: it does not elapse nor can it be measured with the world and all that is therein.

When I learned that my family were present from the moment my husband died and that they participated in his funeral, doing whatever was their duty, I felt a great sense of relief and contentment.

After my family's visit, I recalled the vision that Allah had favoured me with when I had seen the Prophet (peace be upon him) in my sleep. I had noted the date of this vision on the copy of the Qur'an I was reading. When I checked, I found it to be the same as the date of our divorce.

Yes! I had seen the Prophet (peace be upon him) wearing white clothes and behind him Hasan al-Hudaibi also wearing white clothes and a hat. I was standing with 'A'ishah (may Allah be pleased with her) along with a number of other ladies. She was advising me about something when the Prophet (peace be upon him) came up to us, and called: 'Have patience 'A'ishah. Have patience 'A'ishah. Have patience 'A'ishah!'

'A'ishah was pressing my hand, at each utterance, and asked me to be patient.

I related this vision to Hamidah and asked Allah to give me endurance and contentment. I was convinced that a new test was in front of me and asked Allah to bestow His Help, Patience and Firmness on me, for He is the One Who answers prayers.

New Neighbours

One cold, wintry night a commotion could be heard coming from the opposite cell. Salah, the nurse, entered our cell asking for the anti-vomiting medicine that he had given us the previous morning.

He informed us that the person now in the cell opposite was the Prime Minister of Yemen along with another 20 statesmen as well as Shaikh al-'Iryani. We were not surprised, for 'there is nothing new under the sun.'

Did Nasir liberate the Yemen, as his media claimed? With what did he do so?

Did you hear of Britain, when she conquered Egypt, taking tens of men to be imprisoned in London? Did Bonaparte's fleet take the men of Egypt to its prisons in Paris after his crusade of this country?

Nasir Must Stand Trial!

Why, I ask, has Nasir not stood trial for the crimes he has committed, so that Egypt can confront its history with pride? The matter is very serious indeed if Egypt does not wash its hands of the crimes committed during his era. Until this happens, all Egypt will be responsible for his actions with the exception of the Islamic group - the *Ikhwan* - who shouted loudly against him, denouncing his crimes.

The *Ikhwan* were at first deceived by Nasir's movement which they supported. But when they came to know what he and his supporters stood for and to whom its allegiance was directed, they decided to resist it with full *iman*. Thus were the battles of honour waged between right and falsehood from 1954 to 1965. Indeed, the battle of 1965 was a battle of honour and glory, for the rise of Islam as a strong, and lofty power was assured. That despot had thought that the *Ikhwan*'s mission had become

170

history, forgotten, after putting its leaders, and its followers, behind bars.

The battle of 1965 saw the rise of a generation, born in the days of Nasir's *coup*, but absorbed in our mission, engaged in the call to Islam. Nasir could not swallow this; a man and a woman had stripped him, so he said, of his generation. The man was 'Abd al-Fattah Isma'il and the woman was me.

Indeed, we had stripped him of that generation of young people, bringing them up as we had for Islam. It was a battle that cost us some of the dearest men of *da'wah*: Sayyid Qutb, the *Imam* and jurist, 'Abd al-Fattah Isma'il, a man in an *ummah* and an *ummah* in a man, and Muhammad Hawash, that giant in *da'wah* and its understanding.

The days of the military prison were over, but the *Ikhwan* continued to stand like high mountains with all their honour and glory. As for Nasir, he recorded, in history, his disgrace when his soldiers took us, on the 5th June, from military to civilian prisons.

Yes, the 5th June 1967 will long be remembered for its shame and disgrace. With these deeds will Nasir be crowned on the Day of Judgement. With these actions will the Pharaoh of the twentieth century, who transgressed on earth and spread so much corruption among people, be chained.

Notes and References

1. *Al 'Imran*: 139.

2. *Ibid.*: 110.

3. *Al-Saff*: 8.

4/5. *Firdaus* and *'Iliyin* are Qur'anic appellations for two dwellings in Paradise of highest status and rank.

6. *Al-Ra'd*: 28.

7. *Al-Baqarah*: 156.

8. The official authorized to perform acts of marriage and divorce.

CHAPTER 7

In al-Qanatir Prison 5th June

On the 3rd and 4th June our cell door was repeatedly opened without any obvious reason. We were asked if we needed anything, and then subjected to monologues about war and the greatness of the one calling for the liberation of Palestine and the Arabs.

On one occasion, our visitor was the prison doctor, so I decided to ask him what all the furore was about: 'Are we going to liberate Palestine?'

His face turned red with anger. 'What do you mean?', he asked.

'The crucial factor is the result and the extent which the despots hold for Israel in terms of enmity, friendship or treason. As long as International Zionism controls the two superpowers, the rulers of these two will have no choice but to do what it dictates. Palestine will not be liberated except by Islam. The day Islam rules, Palestine will be liberated!'

Surprisingly, our cell door was not opened on the morning of 5th June, but later on a guard suddenly burst in, shouting: 'Nasir has triumphed you B..........!'

He was followed a few moments later by another soldier who came to report to us the news of victory, and of the scores of planes which had been brought down. A third came to relate news about the great leader and his victory, followed by a fourth and a fifth, and so on. All the while we remained silent.

At the time of *'Asr adhan*, Safwat al-Rubi arrived clearly set on causing mayhem. He began to kick me violently with his heavy field boots, then he held me against the wall, beating me against it.

'We've won you B......!'

Hamidah begged him to stop, asking why he was doing this, but the vile beast paid not the slightest attention to her, and persisted in his beating until I passed out. He called for his aides to throw our belongings out of the cell, after which he returned to beat me still more. We were taken out accompanied by his swearing and cursing: 'We've won, we've won despite you, and your hour has come right now.'

That was in the afternoon of 5th June, 1967. Hamidah and I were taken in an armoured lorry packed with officers and soldiers to our new prison. But with Safwat's repeated beatings I was convinced the hour of our own execution had arrived. Time and time again, I repeated to myself: 'Allah is Sufficient unto us and He is the best Disposer of affairs! (*Allah has purchased of the believers their persons and their goods; for theirs (in return) is the Garden (of Paradise) . . .*)[1] and (*We granted not to any man before you permanent life . . .*).'[2]

Suddenly the lorry stopped, and Hamidah shook me to wake me from my trance. I opened my eyes to find we were in front of al-Qanatir prison for women.

The Nightmare

It was night-time. Once inside the prison, we were taken to the governor's office, where our belongings were checked meticulously, and a second check carried

174

out just for good measure. Then to an adjacent room
where we were handed our new prison uniforms, and
then to our cell. What a humiliating, dilapidated affair it
was, with scattered iron bars instead of a proper door, a
bunk-bed, the lower part broken, the upper part with
just one flimsy pillow. The cell itself gave out onto a hall
containing three wards of female prisoners, most of them
convicted of serious crimes ranging from theft to drug
dealing, prostitution and even murder.

We heard the *Adhan* of *'Isha*, so made *tayammum* and
prayed. We tried to sleep, but found it impossible.

Night had spread its hold on the place and the darkness
covered it with forlornness. Our fellow inmates' souls
were clearly saturated with depravity and the wards
locked in the evil they contained. Humanity here had
sunk to the lowest of the low.

We spent the long hours of that night in the incantation
of Allah, remembering Him, glorifying Him and reading:
(. . . *for without doubt in the remembrance of Allah do hearts
find satisfaction*).[3] No sooner had the light of dawn broke
than tranquillity was infused in our beings. We begged
Allah, the Exalted, to relieve us and make, for us, a way
out of this.

What had happened to us whilst in the Military prison
in terms of humiliation, floggings, beatings, executions
and starvation was nothing compared to what we were
witnessing on our first night in this prison. Here we
were in front of a straying herd lost in the dungeons of
Jahiliyyah. Women who claimed to be liberated, were
rather slaves to whims and desires. Their crimes had
submerged them entirely and they had forgotten their
humanity, purity, honour and dignity. Nothing but
animals with no meaning to their lives except eating and
intercourse. Blind animals led by blind men on a road
which zigzagged endlessly in front of them. Those who
want corruption on earth, the people of atheism and

175

falsehood, of evil and crime, had helped these women to sink into this abyss of profanity. The call to *Fajr* prayer was the only thing to break this electrified atmosphere of evil, injustice and darkness. We headed towards the Merciful, the Compassionate, praying and asking Him for His pleasure and relief.

When the wards opened, I immediately asked a prison officer to let me see the governor. A few hours later she escorted me to his office.

A New Kind of Trial

Once in his office the governor delivered his regime: 'You are not allowed to go to the canteen nor are you allowed to have visitors. In short, you don't have any of the rights other prisoners have, at least until we receive new orders, understood!'

'We haven't asked to see you about this matter, but rather to ask you . . .'

'You asked to see me?'

'Yes! We want to change our cell.'

Hamidah added: 'We want a cell with a door and not a cage contraption suitable only for animals!'

'What is this? You'll be returned to the military prison for more of what you already know, so shut up.'

'We cannot stay in a place that does not even befit animals.'

'I am the governor, this is a prison and you are prisoners. Other than this there is nothing which concerns you.' At this he stood up, shouting: 'Please leave!'

'No. We'll stay in here for we'll never return to that cell. Let whatever happens, happen!'

'A prison is a prison, if you don't execute our orders we'll shoot you on the spot!'

'Death is better for us than this kind of life, and besides, life decrees are in the hands of Allah. Our death at your hands is martyrdom.'

He pushed us out of his office and left us in an adjacent room. A little while later a prison officer, Su'ad, took us to what was called an attention-point, a vast ward containing some twenty beds. We were told to follow the officer in charge for it was now income time; we did not at first understand what she meant. We were made to stand in a row of women called the income; a herd of lost and depraved creatures void of all values and ideals.

The prison officer, standing at the door, shouted: 'The income today is 45: 25 begging, 15 prostitution, 3 theft, 2 politicians . . .' She meant, by 'politicians', myself and Hamidah.

We immediately moved away.

'Where are you going? Wait 'til your turn comes.'

'We'll stand separately, we don't belong to this income', I replied.

'What are you saying?'

'We'll stand alone.'

'Aren't these Allah's creatures like you?'

When I did not reply, she began taking the other prisoners into the ward.

'The doctor has asked that you wait until she finishes with the others and then she'll see you', we were told.

The doctor asked us our names, ages and any ailments, and then we were taken to a room and locked up. Shortly afterwards we heard screaming and wailing, and when we asked what was going on, we were informed that it was 'the set-back' (naksah).

I wonder what set-back that could be? Who is to help you, O you poor people? How recurrent are your set-backs! How formidable they are! How deep and cruel too! Set-back after set-back has afflicted our people: a set-back of morals, a set-back of men who rule only with the sword, a set-back of this and of that and, finally, the 5th of June. The colonization of an Arab land, and the rule of its people by violence and crime.

What is this reality that we are living and facing? Islam, the symbol of force, loftiness and dignity, is constantly being suppressed, its children unable to survive, killed off one by one. Unable to smell Islam's breeze or grow, albeit gradually. They kill Islam and its men and along with it all dignity. It is through Islam that loftiness and dignity rise on earth and through which humanity heads towards its Lord in submission and worship, breathing obedience and contentment on the way and answering the call of truth regardless of attendant sacrifices and duties.

These set-backs are the result of your having left Allah's Book behind your backs, forgotten. By Allah! Had we supported His cause, He would have supported us. Had we fully submitted our faces and hearts to Him, by following His upright revelation and straight path, by rushing to what pleases Him and turning away from what displeases Him, He would have supported us. Had we aided Allah's cause, He would have facilitated our rule on earth as His representatives. He would have helped us to defeat the forces of falsehood on this earth. It is with Allah's Book and the *Sunnah* of His Prophet that you triumph and rule the earth and be happy. It is in Allah's obedience that you find dignity, happiness, victory, and the Gardens of Paradise. (. . . *if you will aid (the cause of) Allah, He will aid you, and plant your feet firmly.*)[4] The Caliph 'Umar (may Allah be pleased with him), said: '. . . Allah aids the Muslims by the disobedience of their enemies to Him. Had it been otherwise, we would not have had a chance against them. For our numbers cannot be compared to theirs nor are our armours and equipments comparable to theirs. So if we are equal in disobedience to Allah they will excel us in strength . . .' Indeed, it is because of your departure

178

from the Qur'an and the *Sunnah* that you are defeated, miserable and sinking in your set-backs. For there is nothing in disobeying Allah except humiliation, misery, defeat, weakness, fire and an everlasting punishment. (*'But whosoever turns away from My message, verily for him is life narrowed down, and We shall raise him up blind on the Day of Judgement.' He will say: 'O my Lord! Why have You raised me up blind, while I had sight (before)?' (Allah) will say: 'Thus did you, when Our Signs came to you, disregard them: so will you, this day, be disregarded.' ('And thus do We recompense him who transgresses beyond bounds and believes not in the Signs of his Lord: and the penalty of the Hereafter is far more grievous and more enduring.'*)[5]

My thoughts were interrupted by Hamidah calling me. Sitting near to her in that locked cell, I could still hear the crying and screaming of the defenders of Islam!

We remained in this locked room, that was rarely opened, not knowing a thing about what was happening outside. One day however, we managed to acquire a carton of cigarettes from a prison officer. This became a magical key, turning our harsh prison officer into a docile being. Now we were allowed to have our cell open for a little longer and had news of what was going on around us.

In a nearby cell was a woman with a baby that knew no father, and a little way along another suffering from tuberculosis, living her last days because of her bad behaviour. Near her was a vast ward containing people with different chronic, contagious diseases, and at the bottom of that ward were toilets which we were permitted to share with these sick specimens of humanity, and their behavioural and contagious diseases. In another part of the building were women, whose nationality was not known to us, who enjoyed a clean, furnished and decorated room, with access to a clean toilet. We knew all this because everyone called that part of the prison the 'Hilton'.

We asked the prison officer to allow us to use that other toilet, because of its cleanliness and because we were subjected to such foul language when passing through the ward to use the one allocated to us.

'That other toilet is only for the use of the doctor and the Jews.'

'Did you say Jews?'

'Yes, Jewish ladies: Madam Marcel and Madam Lucy. They are there as if on holiday, no one says a bad thing to them or refuses them anything. It is as if they were at home, maybe even slightly better off. They are accused of spying. Speak with the doctor, she may allow you to use their toilet!'

However, after discussing the matter with the governor, he refused to allow us to use the toilet under the pretext that it was reserved for Jews!

Enemies With Humanity

We delegated our affairs to Allah, the Exalted, and busied ourselves with reading the Qur'an. One day whilst sharing those divine moments with Hamidah, a tall, blond lady entered our cell, and after greeting us asked me: 'Are you Madam Zainab al-Ghazali?'

'Yes', I replied.

'I'm Mrs. Marcel. I'm a political prisoner, although of course there's a difference of beliefs between us: I'm a Jew and you are a Muslim, however people should not lack humanity and especially in times of hardship. There is nothing to stop us enjoying a good relationship in prison even if outside prison there is nothing but war and conflicting aims between us. But here we are all prisoners. I came here behind the officers' backs to offer my help to you.'

We thanked her, and she continued: 'We have some food privileges, and even though these are very limited we would be happy to share what we have with you. I'll make sure it doesn't contain anything unlawful in your religion. Besides, we Jews, like you, don't eat pork.'

As the days passed, Mrs. Marcel brought food for us and, what was more important, she obtained permission for us to use their toilet.

Hamidah felt some vexation at all this, so I told her that Allah, the Exalted, brings good things to His slaves through whomever He wishes. Allah does not exhaust His slaves, nor does He maintain the hardship inflicted on them. In any case we did not have any choice but to cohabit with humanity wherever it exists as long as this cohabitation is within the framework of Islam.

In that scary jungle, in that arid, desolate desert other encounters also lifted our spirits. For example, a humane Christian doctor helped us from time to time, and another good-hearted prisoner gave us tips on how to survive in this wasted place. Everything, she explained, is bought with money. Opening cells for longer periods is bought with money; going out for fresh air is bought with money; food and clothing need money. Everyone here, prisoner and officer alike, has an open mouth ready to swallow what it can. All that was required was money and effort, though these were in any case not easy to achieve.

Death and the Despot!

Despots may forget or try to forget that they have to drink from the cup of death, the cup of return to Allah, the Exalted One. In their forgetfulness they transgress, oppress, torture and inflict all manner of violence on people. They do all this while the wheel of life turns with the will of the Mighty One: day succeeds night, generations are born while others perish, bodies decay and spirits are extracted and no-one can do anything about it.

181

'(*Then why do you not (intervene) when (the soul of the dying man) reaches the throat. And you the while (sit) looking on, - But We are nearer to him than you and yet see not, - then why do you not if you are exempt from (future) account, - call back the soul if you are true (in your claim of Independence).)*'[6]

In the midst of this overcrowded profanity, we learned of Nasir's death. Throughout the prison, everyone was saddened, demonstrative in their wailings.

Allah knows that we do not gloat about the death of anyone, for life's decrees are limited by God and no-one can live more or less than what He prescribes. Yet death is a warning for humanity, a sign for its peril: 'Wake up from your sleep and leave your transgression and despotism, for they won't avail you. [One day] you will leave your transgression and despotism, your wealth and rank, soldiers and party, children and family, you will leave all these behind and be raised in front of Allah, naked and barefoot, as when your mothers conceived you!'

'(. . . *if you could but see how the wicked (do fare) in the flood of confusion at death! - the angels stretch forth their hands, (saying): "Yield up your souls: this day shall you receive your reward, - a penalty of shame, for you told lies against Allah, and scornfully rejected His Signs!" "And behold! You come to Us bare and alone as We created you for the first time: you have left behind you all (the favours) which We bestowed on you: We see not with you your intercessors whom you thought to be partners in your affairs: so now all relations between you have been cut off, and your (pet) fancies have left you in the lurch!")*'[7] (*It was not We that wronged them: they wronged their own souls: the deities, other than Allah, whom they invoked, profited them no whit when the decree of your Lord was issued: nor did they add aught (to their lot) but perdition! Such is the chastisement of your Lord when He chastises communities in the midst of their wrong: grievous, indeed, and severe is His chastisement. In that is a sign for*

182

those who fear the Penalty of the Hereafter: That is a Day for which mankind will be gathered together: that will be a day of Testimony. Nor shall We delay it but for a term appointed. The day it arrives no soul shall speak except by His leave: of those (gathered) some will be wretched and some will be blessed. Those who are wretched shall be in the Fire: there will be for them therein (nothing but) the heaving of sighs and sobs . . . for your Lord is the sure Accomplisher of what He plans. And those who are blessed shall be in the Garden: they will dwell therein for all that time that the heavens and the earth endure, except as your Lord wills: a gift without break) (Hud: 101-8).

A man's death and his return to his Lord do not occupy the minds of the faithful who call for their Lord. Death is a truth which does not distract them. For all that they seek is to live in obedience to Allah, in the precincts of His pleasure and to give their lives and wealth for the sake of spreading *Tawhid.* When their hour, or other people's hour, comes, they will all go to the abode of accountability whereby there is reward or punishment.

Islam's battle is not a battle against an individual or individuals, but a battle of truth against falsehood, a battle of faith against disbelief, a battle of bondage to Allah, alone against the forces of polytheism, atheism and paganism.

The person who dies dies, and the one who is killed is killed, but the faithful who are killed are in Paradise, in the highest *Firdaus (in the assembly of truth, in the Presence of a Sovereign Omnipotent),*[8] martyrs and alive.

(My devotees! No fear shall be on you that Day, nor shall you grieve, - (Being) those who have believed in Our Signs and bowed (their wills to Ours) in Islam. Enter you the Garden, you and your wives in (beauty and) rejoicing. To them will be passed round, dishes and goblets of gold: there will be there all that the souls could desire, all that the eyes could delight in: and you shall abide therein. Such will be the garden of which you are made heirs for your (good) deeds (in

*life). You shall have therein abundance of fruit, from which
you shall have satisfaction.)*[9]

As to the dead of disbelief, falsehood and atheism,
they are in Hell-Fire (*And what will explain to you what
Hell-Fire is? Naught does it permit to endure, and naught
does it leave alone*).[10] It scorches faces and bodies (*. . . for
them will be the Fire of Hell: no term shall be determined for
them, so they should die, nor shall its Penalty be lightened for
them. Thus do We reward every ungrateful one! Therein will
they cry aloud (for assistance): 'Our Lord! Bring us out: we
shall work righteousness not the (deeds) we used to do!' - 'Did
We not give you long enough life so that he that would receive
admonition? And (moreover) the warner came to you, so taste
you (the fruits of your deeds): for the wrong-doers there is no
helper').*[11]

Day after day, night after night, Nasir's death was
reported with never-ending crying, screaming, howling
and wailing. We even read a report of a shaykh describing
Nasir as 'the defender of Islam's sanctuary'. That same
shaykh, swore, only a few years earlier in my home, that
whoever calls Nasir 'the defender of Islam's sanctuary' is
a disbeliever, someone who has taken the garment of
Islam from his neck and lost both this world and the
World-to-Come. In these conditions we received the news
of Nasir's death, instead, as would whoever has an iota
of *iman* in his heart (*. . . and soon will the unjust assailants
know what vicissitudes their affairs will take!*)[12]

But the people in al-Qanatir prison spread the word
that we neither cried nor wailed for the hero of heroes!
For this, they inflicted their wrath on us: how did we
dare not remonstrate for Nasir?

Scum!

(*. . . for the scum disappears like froth cast out; while that
which is for the good of mankind remains on the earth . . .*)[13]

Those hypocrites, those flattering followers who wanted only to serve their earthly masters, did their best to please their superiors. Because of it we suffered harsh treatment and bad manners.

The morning following Nasir's death, a prison officer came into our cell and attacked me with a thick stick. Had it not been for Allah's protection, she would surely have smashed my head open. The prison's administration failed to punish or even reprimand her. She was allowed to move freely about the prison, as if she had done nothing.

When my family came to visit me, I informed them about the incident. They contacted the authorities, large and small, and sent letters to them. The Police began an inquiry, questioned only the prison officer and then informed us she was mentally disturbed.

I asked that the inquiry be halted, and informed the Police that the one who planned the attack was not the prison officer but the forces of atheism and falsehood, believers in crime and violence. There was no sense in punishing someone who had no control over herself and who acted on the instructions of those who plan in the dark, who terrorize the holders of missions and finish them off, (. . . *And Allah has full power and control over His affairs* . . .).[14]

A New Test

The 9th August 1971, was a memorable day bringing us a new test. A prison officer came hastily to me asking that I go and see the prison governor in his office.

I was surprised, and my thoughts wandered, exploring all possibilities. What was happening? What did this despot want from me? Had someone informed the authorities that Hamidah and I were calling to Islam from inside the prison? Had something happened to our

185

relatives? Had we committed an offence without knowing it? Numerous questions flashed through my mind, but still I had no idea what fate had in store for me!

I went to the governor's office, and was told that I was to be released - but alone. I was incredulous; I who had been sentenced to 25 years hard labour was free but my daughter in Islam was to remain alone in this dirty, sinful swamp, alone to bear this endless hardship.

My emotions were mixed, ranging from anger to sadness to outright perplexity.

'No!, No! I will never leave my daughter behind. You are people of devilish planning', I shouted.

The governor asked me to calm down, and explained this was an order that he had received and that he could do nothing about it. I was there by his superiors' orders and I was being released by the same orders. A few moments later, Hamidah was by my side in the office. The governor had called her to calm me down.

It was a tremendous test! How was I to leave Hamidah? How was I to leave her alone in this dark, lonely place, to face harsh treatment? All my being protested, 'No! No! I will not leave her!' But Hamidah said: 'Mother, this is Allah's favour and mercy and all is from Him. Allah does not forget His slaves.'

The governor asked Hamidah to say goodbye and return to her cell. In moments that passed by like the speed of light, Hamidah kissed me and we embraced, tears running down our cheeks. Then, I was alone in the governor's office, completing the formalities for my release. My heart was torn apart, my tears unstoppable.

The Last Bargain

The lorry taking me home suddenly changed direction. I found myself in front of the Secret Service's building.

Again I was locked in a room, from noon to 9 p.m. Then, at last, I was taken to an office where two officers asked me questions about Islam and whether I would be visiting the *Ikhwan* or not.

My mind, my being, was still with my daughter Hamidah. I remonstrated with them that it was unfair that I should be released from my sentence and not her: 'You are people who want evil but Allah will not let you realize what you want!'

'Calm down *Hajjah*!'

'You are planning something evil but Allah is surrounding you and He has control and power over His affairs but most people do not know.'

'These are orders that came from above, we cannot release anyone and we don't have a say in anything!'

Afterwards, I was taken to Ahmad Rushdi's office. Rushdi who had used his whips and sickness against men whom Allah had strengthened their hearts with the ties of faith. I was asked to sit, while he congratulated me on my release. Our discussion was nothing but a series of orders which he wanted me to comply with. Namely, I was not to participate in any Islamic activity, nor was I to visit any of my brothers and acquaintances in Allah, nor was I to co-operate with any of them. Furthermore, I would be obliged to see him in his office from time to time.

When he had finished his instructions, I advised him: 'I reject all what you have said, in fact I reject my release. Inform your superiors, I want to be returned immediately to al-Qanatir prison!'

Rushdi smiled and ended the meeting, saying: 'Anyhow, there are many *Ikhwan* members who have already agreed with me about this . . .'

'By Allah, I don't know anything about the *Ikhwan* except good things. As to what you say about some *Ikhwan*, I cannot comment. I don't believe they promised you anything of the sort. The *Ikhwan* are inheritors of truth, and they work for this truth day and night until Allah brings His victory or they die for His sake.'

The phone rang. Rushdi informed me that my brother, 'Abd al-Mun'im al-Ghazali had arrived. My brother embraced me with tears in his eyes.

'I want you to act as referee between me and the *Hajjah*, for we are at loggerheads', Rushdi said to my brother.

'The *Hajjah* is older than me; I am her youngest brother. It is not my habit to argue with her. Besides, as you know, she has a strong discursive faculty and sound logic.'

'Alright *Hajjah*, congratulations, but make sure that you don't have anything to do with *Ikhwan* military organizations.'

'Secret organizations are your fabrication. The establishment of an Islamic state is an obligation on Muslims and their equipment for it is the call to Allah in the same manner the Prophet (peace be upon him) and his Companions called to Him. This is the mission of every Muslim whether they are from the *Ikhwan* or not.'

With that, I headed, with my brother, towards home. It was 3:00 a.m. on the 10th August 1971.

References

1. *Al-Tawbah*: 111.

2. *Al-Anbiya'*: 34.

3. *Al-Ra'd*: 28.

4. *Muhammad*: 7.

5. *Ta-Ha*: 124-7.

6. *Al-Waqi'ah*: 83-7.

7. *Al-An'am*: 93-4.

8. *Al-Qamar*: 55.

9. *Al-Zukhruf*: 68-73.

10. *Al-Muddaththir*: 27-8.

11. *Fatir*: 36-7.

12. *Al-Shu'ara'*: 227.

13. *Al-Ra'd*: 17.

14. *Yusuf*: 21.

Saybrook 8:40
New London 9:05
Westerly 9:25
Kingston 9:40
Providence 10:00